Ninja Foodi Cookbook UK:

Easy & Delicious Ninja Foodi Recipes Using European Measurements

Daniel Rowley

ISBN-13 : 979-8738377013

Table Of Contents

INTRODUCTION

There is a new darling around!

There is an awesome new gadget out there, and also it is the soulmate of numerous cooks at the moment. There are lots of brand-new devices in the marketplace, and I make sure you need to be questioning what kind of tool it is that has recorded the heart of a great deal of chefs. Well, await it...

It is called the Ninja Foodi, as well as it is an appliance that has responded to the prayers and also needs of lots of cooks on the market, and the solution it provides is merely mind blowing. What is even more, it answers the prayers in a basic yet unmatched means.

A great deal of individuals that use the pressure cooker additionally generally have the demand for an air fryer. These two gadgets are incredible devices in their own right, they have whatever-- virtually every little thing-- that a modern-day chef wants. Multi stoves and also instant pots are likewise extremely crucial appliances for many individuals in this age. It is great to possess all these home appliances, they make the process of preparing a lot of recipes extremely simple and tension cost-free. However, it is stressful and also pricey to get most of these devices, it is really pricey likewise. While the expense of these home appliances does not trouble some people, the anxiety of possessing lots of appliances, as well as the room to maintain the devices will absolutely bother them.

This is where the awesomeness of the Ninja Foodi comes in; imagine a home appliance that is a combination of every little thing we have pointed out over, as well as a lot more. Yes, that is the Ninja Foodi. With this home appliance, you obtain the pressure stove, air fryer, multi cooker, and so on put into one.

What is a Pressure Cooker?

It is very easy often, particularly while composing a publication, to think that all your readers have a basic understanding and also knowledge of what you are claiming, for that reason not taking enough time to go through the concepts. That presumption would not be made right here, as well as because of that, we will certainly slide directly right into discussing what all these cookers and also pots imply.

A pressure cooker is just like the name indicates, it is suggested to pressure cook. I understand that is an extremely circular definition, but that is primarily what a pressure cooker does, it chefs with stress. Discussed simply, it is process of making use of water, or any kind of liquid, to prepare food, in a secured vessel. While utilizing a pressure stove, the heavy steam generated from the boiling water-- or any type of liquid placed in it-- is entraped. The trapped heavy steam is after that made use of to create a raised interior pressure and temperature. The entire concept of a pressure stove is that it is sealed, as well as vapor is not allowed to get away, the vapor created pressure as well as it remains in turn made use of to prepare the food faster and also extra conveniently.

When the pressure cooker was initial designed, it was a revolutionary innovation. For a great deal of people, it was unbelievable that they could get a gadget that would make cooking faster as well as simpler. Prior to the creation of the pressure in cooker, there were several comparable stoves that were designed, these stoves worked as the structure that would ultimately bring about the creation of the stress cookerThis innovation resulted in the beginning of a competitive market of suppliers attempting to generate the very best stress stoves.

Throughout the years, the shape, dimension and also functions of the pressure cookers have transformed and gotten sophisticated. While very little has actually changed about the size-- it varies in sizes, as well as the dimensions of the earlier stoves are not very various from the contemporary ones-- the procedure has transformed a lot. Pressure stoves have experienced generations of use and also consistent upgrade. Each upgrade making it less complicated to use, and also including new modern technology.

Air fryer Specialties

Traditionally, when people wish to fry they need to submerge the food, or any things that will be fried, in hot oil. However, with the air fryer, warm air is flowed around the food via making use of convection system. Unlike the standard system of frying, the air fryer uses very little oil, as well as it distributes air heated up to 200 0 C (392 0F). A normal contemporary air fryer has the ability to fry whatever that can be fried anything that can be fried through the standard frying technique. Occasionally, the air fryer makes use of no oil in all, it depends upon what you are frying as well as what the recipe states.

Pressure cooking and air baking are the two essential functions of the Ninja Foodi, nevertheless, it additionally slow chefs, it steams, it dries out, as well as does a selection of other things. The capability of the Ninja Foodi to combine all these things, that usually take a separate device of their own, is the reason why the Ninja Foodi is so special. Imagine being a cook, or simply a routine chef, that has the need for a pressure cooker and an air fryer; the stress and anxiety of needing to handle the two large appliances as well as the trouble they would certainly trigger when you need to move them about. With the Ninja, you only have to handle one home appliance.

Why the Ninja Foodi?

When a great deal of individuals listen to making use of words 'Ninja', they consider Japanese martial musicians. Practically quickly also, they begin to believe that the Ninja Foodi is a referral to the sort of food the Ninja martial musicians consume; this is extremely much from what the Ninja Foodi is. Other individuals begin to believe it is a referral to Nigerian recipes-- which are constantly extremely positive to consume. I virtually made the very same blunder of attempting to connect it to various other points, it was a shock when I was familiar with that it is not also a type of meal or a dish, it is a device. The most significant shock came when I learnt more about what the gadget does; an air fryer and also a stress stove put right into one!

Let's talk now on the various other attributes of the Ninja Foodi.

The Ninja Foodi remains in its very first generation of manufacturing, the very first collection of the Ninja Foodi were turned out in 2018. It is a huge home appliance, yet absolutely nothing much less is actually to be gotten out of a home appliance that does the job of 2. While it is larger that your regular stress stove or air fryer, it is most definitely not as hefty as both created. It allows in dimension also, it has to do with 13-inches high, regarding 17-inches broad, and also 13-and-a-quarter-inches deep. The weight of the Ninja Foodi is placed at 30.8 extra pounds. All these program that it is not an item that you can move quickly. If you are attempting to obtain it, you will most likely require to develop a room for it in your cooking area. Nevertheless, the room it takes can not be contrasted to that which an immediate pot stress stove as well as an air fryer would certainly take. Additionally, it is really crucial that you develop an area that is really near an electric outlet, since the size of the electric cable is just 33 inches long, and also it is mentioned plainly in the guidebook that it need to not be made use of along with an expansion cable.

The Ninja Foodi includes 2 different covers; one for stress food preparation and also the various other for air frying. I understand a great deal of individuals are normally shocked when they listen to that within a solitary pot, you can press chef as well as additionally air fry, yet this is implemented due to both covers that feature the device. Initially, you have the air frying cover which is completely affixed to the Foodi, and also it can not be removed for whatever factor. Second, you have the stress food preparation cover, which is removable. Relying on the type of feature you are attempting to utilize, each cover would certainly be picked to fit your food preparation demand. If you are stress food preparation, the air frying cover keeps up, as well as it stays like that till you are via with your stress food preparation. The reality that air frying cover remains open, also when not being used, can make the stress stove show up a little unpleasant when being used; and also it has actually been a large issue for a great deal of individuals.

The air frying cover looks much like a typical air frying cover, as well as the stress food preparation cover resembles that of the instantaneous pot. Primarily, the covers are one of the most essential components, they are what produce the difference in between the air fryer and also the stress stove. If you try to press chef, while you have the air frying cover on, the stove will certainly not begin, it will certainly inform you to place the ideal cover on. This additionally functions as a kind of security for individuals that might not recognize exactly how the home appliance functions actually. On the stress food preparation cover, there is a red flip bell/ pin, as well as the stress launch bell. The stress launch bell has the air vent as well as the seal choice. Much like a regular stress stove, the air vent choice enables you to launch the stress that has to the stove has to have developed.

The Ninja Foodi is extremely simple to utilize. This, possibly, is the best feature of the home appliance. Typically, when a new appliance hits the marketplace, users need to start learning its operation slowly. Nonetheless, with the Ninja Foodi, it is very simple to utilize, as well as the user handbook that comes with it makes it also easier. For individuals who have made use of the instant pot, or any kind of stress cooker formerly, using the Ninja Foodi is nearly like utilizing any one of these devices. Nevertheless, for those that have no anticipation of exactly how to push chef, it is advised by Ninja that you take a brief trial run with water. Taking the brief test will assist you how it is done, and also it will certainly assist you loosen up any anxiety you might have concerning using it, because, a lot of people really get distressed when trying out a brand-new appliance-- I kid you not. As claimed earlier, the functions on the Ninja Foodi, are the functions you would certainly discover on your stress stove or your air fryer.

The Ninja Foodi comes in two groups, and also the rates of the two differ. Alongside with the cost being various, they also include slightly various devices. The various groups as well as designs of the Ninja should be noted before heading out to obtain one, this will help you recognize which to choose as well as which not to choose. In this book, I will assist you by making the process of making a decision which to get simpler by explaining each one. What need to notify your choice, nonetheless, is what you require it for. If for example you do not dehydrate, after that it is no usage getting the model that comes with the drying out function.

What is in package? I make certain this is a question would certainly enjoy addressed. There are lots of unboxing video clips that can be seen online, yet here are the standard things you will certainly find in package.

Past the significant differences that you receive from purchasing various designs, there are some continuous accessories that come with all the devices, irrespective of the model.
1. The initial is the guidebook-- naturally, every device features a manual.

2. The second point that you would certainly locate in your Ninja Foodi, regardless of the design, is both covers. As specified previously, there is a separate lid for stress cooking and air baking; both covers permit it to be able to carry out the actions easily. The air frying lid is attached completely, while the pressure food preparation lid is detachable.

3. A ceramic nonstick pot. The Ninja Foodi comes with a 6 and a half quart detachable food preparation pot, with markings inside-- in mugs and also meters-- that make it very easy to gauge; the pot has two 'max' lines, one for general food preparation, as well as the other for stress food preparation. The nonstick attribute implies that your food does not stick to the pot, and also it likewise makes it very easy to clean. When using the pot, it is a good idea not to make use of a metal tool, as it might damage the surface area of the pot. Without the pot, the Foodi can not be made use of. The Foodi is just turned on for use when the pot touches the surface of home appliance.

4. A chef as well as crisp rack basket. The basket can be made use of when you are trying to use the tender crisp choice. The basket has a diffuser at the bottom that facilitates as well as possible for whatever you are cooking to be evenly cooked. The diffuser can be easily detached, and that makes it really easy to tidy.

5. A chef as well as crisp shelf. Just like the basket, the shelf can be utilized when you are attempting to use the tender crisp choice. The rack is an extremely beneficial accessory since it is relatively easy to fix; it has low and high placements. You can switch over between both settings, depending upon what you are cooking and also just how you want it cooked.

6. It includes a cook publication, or an overview, if you like, with regarding 45+ recipes that can be made with the Ninja Foodi.

The stress food preparation as well as the air frying choice have different features, and also the various options end up being triggered when the corresponding attribute is being utilized. For example, you can not bake unless the air crisping lid is on.

On the screen of the Ninja Foodi, there are numerous functions. Even though these features are easy to use and also direct, they need to be grasped nevertheless.

1. Much like any kind of various other stress stove, the Ninja Foodi has the temperature level and the time function. The temperature function is written as "TEMPERATURE", while the moment function is written conventionally as "TIME". The time checks out in hour, minutes and also seconds only. If you are cooking for over a hr, the hour reviews to your left, while the min reads to your right. If you are preparing for much less than a hr, the minute checks out to your left, and also the second to your right. The

temperature level can either go up or down, nevertheless, there are set numbers that you can not exceed or listed below.

2. Simply in between the time as well as temperature, you have the time/temperature display. This display shows you the temperature level as you attempt to adjust it, and it shows you the moment. The good thing is that it does not only show the moment, it also counts down to the moment you have established. If for example, you establish it to pressure cook for just 15 minutes, the time begins to count down, such that you can easily monitor the moment. The very best component, however, is that the moment the countdown is done, the Ninja stops stress cooking immediately.

3. Directly under the time/temperature screen, there are two icons; one standing for the pressure cooking choice, while the other represents the air crisping alternative. The icon to the left has what looks like a vapor, as a result it stands for the pressure food preparation feature, while the image to the right represents the air crisping choice. When the stress cooker is being made use of, the stress food preparation symbol begins, and it shows a blue color. Similarly, the air crisping sign comes on when the air crisping alternative is being used, as well as it reveals a red color.

4. Straight the underneath both signs, there is the "FEATURE". The feature includes all things that the Ninja can do, and it is separated into two categories. The initial classification has the complying with features;

i.PRESSURE
ii.STEAM
iii.SLOW CHEF
iv.SEAR/ SAUTE.

The 2nd group is the "TENDERCRISP". This group includes the complying with functions.

i.AIR CRISP.
ii.BAKE/ ROAST.
iii.BROIL.
iv.DEHYDRATE.

All things that the Ninja Foodi can do are included in both categories that we have actually detailed above. For any person that is either curious about pressure cooking, slow-moving cooking or air crisping/frying, this appliance is the ideal tool for them. As stated previously, the way it is set up methods that totally various options can not be mistaken with each or other or confused. For instance, someone that intends to air crisp or broil can not make the blunder of slow cooking or stress food preparation, this is since the features only respond to appropriated covers, the air crisping option will certainly not deal with the stress food preparation lid on.

5. After the features, we have the "keep cozy" option, the start/stop button, and the power button. The keep cozy choice is suggested to keep your food-- or whatever you have in the Foodi-- warm for approximately twelve hrs. As explained earlier, the Ninja Foodi is set up to stop the minute the time you establish is full. The Foodi quiting immediately means that you can be sure that even in your absence, your food will certainly not prepare beyond the moment you desire it to. After the Foodi stops reviewing the time, it immediately switches on the maintain warm choice, as well as it can stay this way for up to twelve hours. The maintain warm feature is very useful because it can easily be used when you are not ready to take the food out of the Foodi yet.

The start/stop switch and also the power switch are possibly the simplest to use and also easy to identify among all the features of the Foodi. The reality that your Ninja is does not suggest it will begin work yet, it only starts to work when you struck the beginning button, and it quits, when you hit the stop button. Likewise, connecting the cable right into a socket does not mean it has begun obtaining power, it begins to receive power when you struck the power button. For some pressure stoves, the stove begins to function the moment it is connected in.

Likewise, while cooking, a lot of people like to check on what they are cooking, to see how well the food is doing. In this type of situation, it a good idea not to utilize the stop button, since that will certainly clean away the moment that is reading by the Foodi. In such a situation, it is recommended to just open the lid, after that the timer would quit automatically. When you close the cover, the timer would certainly proceed instantly.

Running the Ninja Foodi

Each feature is different, both in form as well as how it functions. The 'stress' option works in different ways from the steam or the broil choice, as a result, the cooking time and also the temperature that can be allowed for each of these functions.

For example, with the "AIR CRISP" function in operation, the default temperature level is 390F, nonetheless, you can choose any temperature level between 300F and 400F. With the air crisp feature, the maximum time you can prepare is one hr (01:00). As discussed previously, with the air crisp feature, you can either utilize the reversible rack or the basket with the diffuser affixed.

With the bake/roast function being used, the default temperature level is 375F, with the option to set between 250F to 400F. The optimal time for cooking time with the bake/roast function is four hrs (04:00). For the broil feature, there is no temperature change, nonetheless, you can establish the moment from any kind of min you want up to thirty minutes. With the broil function, you can utilize the relatively easy to fix shelf.

1. Pressure release valve
2. Reversible rack
3. Crisping lid
4. Digital controls
5. Pressure lid
6. Cook & Crisp™ Basket
7. Cooking pot
8. 14 levels of safety

Already, with the means the Foodi is set up and set up, you can not perhaps fail or make a mistake with it. The truth that they have constraints on the temperature level and time established according to the function you are making use of ways there is perhaps no chance for you to destroy your food or even shed your house down with this appliance. Likewise, it indicates that you do not have to rest by the Foodi for a hr, or till your countdown is up, the Foodi instantly quits when the timer is up, and changes to "keep cozy".

Going on, with the pressure lid on, you can utilize any one of the features under the very first classification, as explained previously, they consist of, pressure, heavy steam, slow-moving cook, sear/saute. When making use of any one of these functions, it is important to include liquid to the pot before you start cooking. Also, it is essential, to note that if you are cooking things like rice or various other foods that broadens or rises, you must not load the pot majority means.

With the stress function on, you can set the temperature level to "HI" or "LO", and also the moment can be readied to up to 4 hours. When using this function, you require a minimum of half a mug of liquid in the pot.

With the heavy steam feature, there is no temperature level modification, but you can establish the time for up to half an hour. With this function, you must make sure that at the very least a cup of liquid is contributed to the pot.

The sluggish cook function enables temperature level change, as well as like the stress feature, you can establish the sluggish chef function to HI or LO. Using the HI temperature level, you can establish your time to anytime from four hrs to twelve hrs. Making use of the LO temperature level setting, you can establish it from six hours to twelve hrs. With the sluggish chef additionally, it is necessary to include liquid, the quantity depends upon what you are cooking.

With the SEAR/SAUTE function, you have more temperature level alternatives than the other three functions, you have the HI, MD: HI, MD, LO, LO: MD. For the SEAR/SAUTE, MD implies medium, for that reason you can pick to be in the middle of HI and LO, and lots of other alternatives affixed to it. For this feature, there is no time change, only the temperature level adjustment.

When you want to make use of the pressure cooking cover, you will need to turn the pressure launch bell to seal. After you have actually clicked the 'begin' switch, a line will certainly begin turning on the screen. The line will certainly remain to revolve until the Foodi pertains to stress, then it will start to count down to the time you have set. The time it will certainly consider the stove to find to pressure depends upon what you are attempting to prepare. What is nearly certain though is that the Ninja Foodi involves push faster than your typical pressure cooker.

The concern a great deal of people that have used the Instantaneous Pot or any various other pressure stove previously would have is that, exists any kind of difference between the Ninja Foodi and any other pressure cooker? This is a really nice inquiry. There are few differences occasionally, however these distinctions are not deal breakers, for that reason they need to not stop you from updating, if you are taking into consideration to.

The first distinction is with the food preparation pot. We are mosting likely to utilize the Instantaneous Pot as our point of comparison in between the two. There is a noticeable difference between the food preparation pot of the Ninja Foodi from that of the Immediate Pot, as an example. The pot of the Foodi is not as high as that of the Instant Pot, yet the pot of the Foodi is wider than that of the Instantaneous Pot. In fact, the cooking pot of the Instant pot would certainly fit comfortably in the cooking of the Foodi.

The second point of difference is with the materials with which the food preparation pots are constructed from. The Instantaneous Pot cooking pot is made of a stainless steel, while the Ninja Foodi is made of a ceramic non stick coating. For every person that has tried the non stick finishing, they definitely choose it to the stainless-steel pot. I have done a substantial explanation on that earlier, which you will find under "Why the Ninja Foodi".

Breakfast

I understand a great deal of people would want recognizing the sort of dishes that can be cooked with the Ninja Foodi. The important things anyone who has used the stress stove or the air fryer in the past want to recognize is if the recipes for the stress cooker can additionally work with the Ninja Foodi. As well as the response is, await it, INDEED! All the dishes for the stress cooker, and also extra, would certainly deal with the Ninja Foodi. So, there is no demand to be scared about the kind of recipe that benefits the Ninja Foodi. As mentioned previously, consisted of in package of the Ninja Foodi is the fifty dish chef publication; the chef publication describes, from start to finish, exactly how to make about fifty recipes with the Ninja Foodi.

Without more trouble, allow us jump into the recipes that you can prepare with the Ninja Foodi.

French Toast Sticks Dish

Serving: 4
Time: Preparation Time: 5mins, Prepare Time: 12mins

Ingredients
- 4 - pieces of sliced up bread
- 2 - Tablespoon of soft butter
- 2 - eggs carefully defeated
- Salt.
- Cinnamon.
- Nutmeg.
- Ground cloves.
- Icing sugar.

Instructions
1. Preheat Air-fryer to 180 * Celsius.

2. In a dish, tenderly defeated with each other two eggs, a sprinkle of salt, a couple of frustrating drinks of cinnamon, and little portions of both nutmeg as well as ground cloves.
3. Spread both sides of bread cuts and cut into strips.
4. Dig each strip in the egg mix as well as manage in Air-fryer.
5. Following 2 mins of cooking, stop the Air-fryer, take out the meal, guaranteeing you place the frying pan on a heat secure surface area, as well as sprinkle the bread with food preparation shower.
6. When you have actually freely covered the strips, flip and spray the second side too.
7. Return skillet to fryer as well as prepare for 4 additional mins, examining following a few mins to guarantee they are cooking equitably as well as not consuming.
8. At the factor when egg is cooked as well as bread is brilliant darker, get rid of from Air-fryer as well as offer immediately.
9. To improvement and serve, spray with icing sugar, top with whip cream, shower with syrup, or existing with a little dish of syrup for diving.
Nourishment Info: Calories 213.8, Fat 7.3 g, Carbs 33.4 g, Sugars 12.2 g, Healthy protein 3.7 g.

Molly's Donuts

Serving: 4
Time: Preparation Time: 10mins, Prepare Time: 20mins

Ingredients
- 1 - can Flaky Layers biscuits Powder
- 3 - tablespoons melted butter
- 1/3 - cup granulated sugar
- 1/2 - to 1 teaspoon cinnamon
- 4 - tablespoons dark brown sugar
- Pinch of allspice

Instructions

1. Join sugar, cinnamon, dark-colored sugar, and allspice in a little (grain or soup measured) dish as well as deposited.
2. Remove bread rolls from a container and use a 1-inch circle bun shaper to get rid of the openings of the prime focus of every roll.
3. Air sears the DONUTS at 350 levels Fahrenheit for 5 minutes.
4. As each bunch of doughnuts as well as openings leaves the fryer, use a baked great brush to repaint margarine over the whole surface of every doughnut and also space.
5. After every doughnut as well as opening is painted with the spread, drop into the dish with the sugar mix and coat totally with the blend.
6. Tenderly get rid of abundance.
7. Offer doughnuts and also openings cozy.
Nutrition Information: Calories 390g, Fat 15g, Carbs 58g, Sugars 24g, Protein 7g

Wholemeal Bread

Servings: 2
Time: Preparation Time: 5mins, Prepare Time: 10mins

Ingredients

- 4 - Slices Wholemeal Bread
- 2 - Big Eggs
- 1/4 - Cup Whole Milk
- 1/4 - Mug Brown Sugar
- 1 - Tbsp Honey
- 1 - Tsp Cinnamon
- Pinch Of Nutmeg
- Pinch Of Icing Sugar

Instructions

1. Cleave up your cuts of bread right into competitors. Each cut must make 4 officers.
2. Spot the rest of your repairings (in addition to the icing sugar) right into a blending dish as well as mix well.

3. Dive each trooper into the mix with the goal that it is all over covered and after that location it into the Air Fryer.
4. When you're established you will certainly have 16 cannon fodders as well as later should all be enjoyable and also wet from the blend.
5. Area on 160c for 10 mins or up until they are positive as well as company like salute and are never again damp. Part of the means with food preparation turn them over with the goal that the two sides of the competitors have a decent possibility to be equally prepared.
6. Present with a sprinkle of topping sugar and also some brand-new berries.
Nutrition Info: Calories 309g, Fat 13.61 g, Carbs 42.25 g, Sugars 26.34 g, Healthy protein 5.15 g.

Cinnamon Rolls

Serving: 8.
Time: Preparation Time: 25mins, Food Preparation Time: 35mins.

Ingredients

- 1 - pound frozen bread dough.
- 1/4 - mug butter.
- 3/4 - mug brownish sugar.
- 1 1/2 - tablespoons ground cinnamon.

Cream Cheese Luster:

- 4 - ounces cream cheese.
- 2 - tablespoons butter.
- 1 1/4 - mugs powdered sugar.
- 1/2 - teaspoon vanilla.

Instructions

1. Offer the bread combination a chance to come to area temperature on the counter. On a naturally floured surface fold the batter into a 13-inch by 11-inch square shape. Position the square form so the 13-inch side is facing you.

2. Consolidate the dark-colored sugar and also cinnamon in a little dish. Spray the blend equitably over the buttered mix, maintaining the 1-inch fringe disclosed. Fold the batter right into a log starting with the side local to you. Roll the combination strongly, making a point to relocate equitably and push out any kind of air pockets. When you get to the exposed side of the batter, press the blend onto the transfer to seal it together.

3. Cut the indication into 8 pieces, cutting slowly with a sawing motion so you do not straighten out the batter. Transform the cuts on their sides and also spread with a clean cooking area towel.

4. To make the coating, position the cream cheddar and also margarine in a microwave-safe bowl. Mollify the blend in the microwave for 30 secs on end until it is anything yet challenging to blend.

5. At the factor when the rolls have increased, preheat the air fryer to 350°F.

6. Exchange 4 of the moves to the air fryer pet crate. Air-broil for 5 minutes. Transform the moves over and air-sear for an extra 4 mins. Rehash with the rest of the 4 rolls.

7. Provide the rolls a possibility to cool for 2 or 3 mins prior to finish. Spread extensive littles cream cheddar coat over the cozy cinnamon rolls, enabling a section of the covering to flow down the side of the rolls. Offer warm and appreciate!

Nutrition Details: Calories 213.8 g, Fat 7.3 g, Carbs 33.4 g, Sugars 12.2 g, Healthy protein 3.7 g.

Hash Browns

Serving: 8
Time: Preparation Time: 15mins, Food Preparation Time: 15mins

Ingredients

- 4 - Huge potatoes
- 2-- tsp. Corn flour
- Salt.
- Pepper powder.
- 2-- tsp. Chili flakes.
- 1-- tsp. Garlic powder.
- 1-- tsp. Onion Powder.
- 2-- tsp. Vegetable Oil.

Instructions

1. Douse the ruined potatoes in infection water. Network the water. Rework the progression to vacant excess starch out of potatoes.

2. In a non-stick skillet heat, 1 tsp of grease and sauté damaged potatoes till cooked somewhat for 3-4mins.

3. Chill it off as well as trade the potatoes to a plate.

4. Consist of corn flour, salt, pepper, garlic, as well as onion powder and stew declines and also integrate generally.

5. Spread over home plate and pat it immovably with your fingers.

6. Cool it for 20 minutes.

7. Preheat air fryer at 180C.

8. Take out the currently cooled potato and separation right into equal pieces with a blade.

9. Brush the cord container of the air fryer with little oil.

10. Identify the hash darker pieces in the container as well as broil for 15 mins at 180C.

11. Take out the cage and flip the hash tans at 6 minutes with the objective that they are air fricasseed constantly.

12. Serve it hot with ketchup.

Nourishment Information: Calories 104.5 g, Fat 0.4 g, Carbs 23.9 g, Sugars 1.5 g, Protein 3g.

Breakfast Sausage

Serving: 7.

Time: Preparation Time: 5mins, Cooking Time: 6mins.

Ingredients
- 8 - Heat N' Serve Sausages.
- 2 - Parts American Cheese.
- 8 - count Refrigerated Crescent Roll Dough.
- 8 - Wood Skewers.
- Syrup, Catsup or BBQ for dipping.

Instructions
1. On a level surface, separate Crescent Rolls.
2. Open up Sausages.
3. Cut Cheese.
4. Area One Crescent Roll ostensibly, unrolled.
5. Work from Wide Triangular to the pointer of the triangle.
6. Include wiener as well as cheddar strip to the best piece of the sickle roll.
7. Pressure each end over frankfurter and cheddar.
8. Roll as well as put the remainder of the blend till you accomplish the pointer of the triangle.
9. Emphasize to squeeze all the batter.
10. Find approximately 4 of these in Air Fryer.
11. Select 380 ° for 3 minutes.
12. Expel as well as consist of stick.
13. Plate and present with BARBEQUE, Ketchup or Syrup for dunking.
Nourishment Information: Calories 413g, Fat 19.5 g, Carbs 54.8 g, Sugars 2.3 g, Protein 4.7 g.

Best Home Fried Potatoes

Servings: 4.
Time: Prep Time: 30mins, Cook Time: 35mins.

Ingredients

- 3 - large Potatoes rubbed.
- 1 - tool Yellow.
- 1 - little Red Pepper diced.
- 2 - Tablespoons Bacon Oil.
- 2 - tsps Sea Salt.
- 1 - teaspoon Onion Powder.
- 1 - tsp Garlic Powder.
- 1 - teaspoon Paprika.

Instructions
1. Spot cleaned/diced potatoes into a big bowl, spread with water as well as sprinkle for 20-30 mins.
2. Integrate without or with spices and established. Oil the bottom of your Air Fryer Basket with Coconut Oil.
3. Channel potatoes, dry well, as well as spot right into big mixing dish.
4. Include Sir Francis Bacon Oil or Oil on your potatoes and blend absolutely. Unload steamed potatoes right into Air Fryer Basket and Drawer/Basket into Air Fryer.
5. Cook potatoes at 370 tiers for 20mins, drinking some circumstances amidst food preparation.
6. Bones onions and red peppers and also place right into blending bowl and deposited until Air Fryer Beeps.
7. At the variable whilst Air Fryer beeps, move potatoes right into a dish with onions/peppers and mix with. Consist of spices and also mix with.
8. Unload blend into Air Fryer Basket and see into the Air Fryer.
9. Prepare at 380 stages for 5-10mins, or till potatoes are scorched and also onions are delicate.
Nutrition Information: Calories 241g, Fat 4g, Carbs 46g, Sugar 21g, Protein 4g.

Cinnamon Toast

Servings: 4.
Time: Prep Time: 5mins, Prepare Time: 5mins.

Ingredients
- 12 - Bread wheat.
- 1 - stick Salted Butter space temperature level.
- 1/2 - mug White Sugar.
- 1 1/2 - tsps Ground Cinnamon.
- 1 1/2 - tsps Pure Vanilla Extract.
- 4-6 - cranks Fresh Ground Black Pepper.

Instructions
1. Extra pound sweetened margarine with a fork or rear of a spoon and include sugar, cinnamon, pepper, and vanilla.
2. Mix to entirely combine.
3. Spread on bread, attempting to entirely cover the whole surface area.
4. Detect the exact same number of cuts suit your Air Fryer.
5. Cook at 400 levels Fahrenheit for 5 mins.
6. Eliminate from Air Fryer as well as reduced edge to corner.

Nutrition Information: Calories 320g, Fat 9g, Carbs 55g, Sugar 29g, Protein 3g.

Tofu Scramble

Servings: 4.
Time: Prep Time: 5mins, Prepare Time: 30mins.

Ingredients
- 1 - block tofu - cut right into.
- 2 - tbsps soy sauce.
- 1 - tablespoon olive oil.
- 1 - teaspoon turmeric extract.
- 1/2 - tsp garlic powder.
- 1/2 - teaspoon onion powder.
- 1/2 - mug cut onion.
- 2 1/2 - cups sliced red potato.
- 1 - tablespoon olive oil.
- 4 - cups broccoli florets.

Instructions

1. In a tool gauged dish, toss together the tofu, soy sauce, olive oil, turmeric, garlic powder, onion powder, and also onion. Put aside to marinate.
2. In a various, little dish, hurl the potatoes in the olive oil, as well as air sear at 400F for 15 mins, shaking when around 7-8 minutes right into cooking.
3. Shake the potatoes one more time, then include the tofu, holding any type of added sauce.
4. Set the tofu and potatoes to prepare at 370 for 15 additional mins, and also start the air fryer.
5. While the tofu is cooking, toss the broccoli in the saved marinade.
6. On the off possibility that it isn't enough to get it everywhere throughout the broccoli, consist of a smidgen of extra soy sauce.
7. Dry broccoli isn't your friend, people. At the point when there are 5 mins of cooking time staying, add the broccoli to the air fryer.

Nutrition Details: Calories 87g, Fat 4.4 g, Carbs 3.4 g, Sugar 2.3 g, Protein 10g.

Breakfast Frittata

Servings: 2
Time: Preparation Time: 10mins, Cooking Time: 15mins

Ingredients
- 3 - eggs
- 1/2 - Italian sausage
- 4 - cherry tomatoes
- 1 - tbsp olive oil
- Cut parsley
- Grano Padano cheese
- Salt/Pepper.

Instructions
1. Preheat the Air-fryer to 360 degrees.

2. Detect the cherry tomatoes and frankfurter in the preparing frill and warm at 360 degrees for 5 mins.

3. In a little dish, blend the rest of the dealings with each other.

4. Eliminate the home heating decoration from the Air-fryer and include the egg blend, ensuring it is also. Get ready for an extra 5 mins.

Nourishment Info: Calories 234.1 g, Fat 12.8 g, Carbs 14.6 g, Sugars 1.3 g, Protein 17.7 g.

Family Sausage Rolls

Serving: 4.
Time: Preparation Time: 20mins, Cook Time: 25mins.

Ingredients

- 225g - Plain Flour.
- 100g - Butter.
- 1 - Tbsp Olive Oil.
- 300g - Sausage Meat.
- 1 - Medium Egg defeated.
- 1 - Tsp Mustard.
- 1 - Tsp Parsley.
- Salt & Pepper.

Instructions

1. Detect the flour, the flavor, and also the spread into a blending dish and also using the combing in strategy, massage the fat right into the flour till you have a blend that appears like bread items. Include the olive oil as well as a little water and using your hands make the blend right into a half-cracked mix.

2. Function the baked good as you integrate it with the goal that it becomes stunning as well as smooth.

3. Reveal the baked excellent onto a worktop and also make a square state of cake. Using a tsp massage the mustard right into the baked good.

4. Spot the hotdog meat in the within as well as clean the edges of the cake with egg. Go up the wiener folds as well as after that partition into sections.

5. Brush the tops and sides of the frankfurter moves with even more eggs.

6. Cut the highest point of the frankfurter moves with a blade so they get the possibility to loosen up.

7. Prepare in the Air-fryer at 160c for 20 minutes and later for a more 5 mins at 200c with the objective that you can have that remarkable crispy baked good.

Nourishment Information: Calories 659g, Fat 45g, Carbs 43g, Sugars 0.3 g, Healthy protein 18g.

Blueberry Lemon Muffins

Servings: 1.
Time: Prep Time: 10mins, Prepare Time: 15mins.

Components

1. In a little dish incorporate oneself climbing flour as well as sugar. Put aside.

2. In a medium dish combine lotion, oil, lemon juice, eggs, and vanilla.

3. Add the flour mix to the liquid mix and also blend just up until blended. Mix in the blueberries.

4. Spoon the player right into silicone cupcake holders, sprinkle 1/2 tsp. dark tinted sugar over every biscuit.

5. Prepare at 320 degrees for 10 minutes, examine biscuits at 6 minutes to ensure they are not cooking exceedingly quick.

6. Place a toothpick into the prime focus of the biscuit and also when the toothpick levels as well as the biscuits have actually prepared they are ended up.

7. No engaging factor to over-heat the biscuits, they will keep food preparation for another minute or 2 after they are expelled from the air fryer.
8. Expel as well as cool down.

Nutrition Details: Calories 279.6 g, Fat 22.3 g, Carbs 2.9 g, Sugars 1.5 g, Protein 16.1 g.

Vegan Wrapped Bacon Mini Burritos

Servings: 4.
Time: Prep Time: 15mins, Cook Time: 30mins.

Ingredients
- 2 tbsps cashew butter.
- 2-- 3 tablespoons tamari.
- 1-- 2 tablespoons liquid smoke.
- 1-2 tbsps water.
- 4 items rice paper.
- 2 portions VeganEgg scramble.
- 1/3 cup roasted sweet potato.
- 8 strips roasted red pepper.
- 1 small tree broccoli, sautéed.
- 6-8 stalks fresh asparagus.
handful spinach, kale, other eco-friendlies.

Instructions
1. Preheat griddle to 350 ° F. Line heating sheet with the material.
2. In a little superficial bowl, whisk together cashew margarine, tamari, fluid smoke, and water. Put aside.
3. Establish all dental fillings to collect rolls.
4. Rice Paper Hydrating Technique: have a large plate/surface prepared to fill/move wrapper.
5. Hold one rice paper immersed component running trendy water, obtaining the two sides of wrapper damp, for only a couple of moments.

6. Get rid of from water as well as keep in mind that still company, put on a plate to fill-- rice paper will certainly decrease as it rests, yet.
7. will not be soft to the point that it adheres to the surface or tears when dealing with.
8. Load by putting correctings simply off from the center, leaving sides of rice paper cost-free.
9. Crease opposite sides in like a burrito, relocation from taking care of side to opposite side and also seal. Plunge each layer right into cashew fluid smoke mix, covering entirely. Coordinate carry on parchment home heating sheet.
10. Prepare at 350 ° F for 15 mins. Eliminate from broiler, pass on, return and keep planning for an extra 10 minutes, up until bacon is fresh. Offer warm.
Nourishment Information: Calories 260g, Fat 17g, Carbs 13.8 g, Sugars 0.3 g, Healthy protein 15.6 g.

Monte Cristo Double-decker

Serves: 1.
Time: Preparation Time: 25mins, Cook Time: 20mins.

Ingredients
- 1 - egg.
- 3 - tbsps heavy cream.
- 1/4 - teaspoon vanilla remove.
- 2 - slices sourdough.
- 2 1/2 - ounces cut Swiss cheese.
- 2 - ounces pieces deli pork.
- 2 - ounces sliced deli turkey.
- 1 - tsp butter.
- powdered sugar.
- raspberry jam.

Instructions
1. Consolidate the egg, lotion and vanilla concentrate in a shallow dish.

2. Detect the bread on the counter. Produce a sandwich with one cut of Swiss cheddar, the ham, the turkey and afterward a second cut of Swiss cheddar on one cut of the bread. Top with the various other cut of bread and also press down marginally to level.

3.Pre-heat the air fryer to 350ºF.

4. Eliminate a little aluminum foil regarding a comparable dimension as the bread as well as brush the foil with the dissolved spread.

5. Plunge both sides of the sandwich in the egg player. Give the player a possibility to splash into bread for around 30 secs on each side.

6. At that point location the sandwich on the lubed aluminum foil and exchange it to the air fryer bushel. For additional sautéing, clean the acme of the sandwich with the softened spread. Air-sear at 350ºF for 10 minutes. Turn the sandwich over, brush with spread and also air-sear for an added 8 mins.

7. Exchange the sandwich to an offering plate and sprinkle with powdered sugar. Present with raspberry or blackberry safeguards as an afterthought.

Nutrition Details: Calories 250g, Fat 16.57 g, Carbs 12.42 g, Sugars 2.84 g, Protein 12.26 g.

Strawberry Pop Tarts

Servings: 6
Time: Prep Time: 15mins, Cook Time: 10mins

Ingredients
- 2 - chilled pie crusts
- 1 - tsp cornstarch
- 1/4 - cup strawberry preserves
- 1/3 - mug plain, non-fat Greek yogurt.
- 2-- oz. cream cheese.
- 1 - tsp sugar sprays.
- 1 - tsp stevia.

- olive oil or coconut oil spray.

Instructions
1. Lay the pie outside layer on a level functioning surface. I made use of a bamboo cutting board.

2. Utilizing a blade or pizza shaper, reduced the 2 pie outside layers right into 6 square shapes. Each should be truly long as you will overlay it over to shut the pop tart.

3. Add the jelly as well as corn starch to a bowl and blend well.

4. Consist of a tablespoon of the jelly to the hull. Spot the jam in the top area of the covering.

5. Fold each over to shut the pop tarts.

6. Utilizing a fork, make inscribes in every one of the pop tarts, to make vertical as well as also lines along the sides.

7. Spot the pop tarts airborne Fryer. Shower with oil. I like to make use of olive oil.

8. Cook on 375 levels for 10 minutes. You might require to check the Pop-Tarts around 8 minutes to guarantee they aren't unreasonably fresh for your appreciating.

9. Settle the Greek yogurt, cream cheddar, as well as stevia in a bowl to make the topping.

10. Allow the Pop Tarts to cool prior to expelling them from the Air Fryer. This is crucial. In the event that you do not allow them to cool down, they may damage.

11. Get rid of the pop tarts from the Air Fryer. Leading each with the icing. Sprinkle sugar sprays all through.

Nutrition Information: Calories 187.3 g, Fat 8.2 g, Carbs 28.7 g, Sugars 0.1 g, Protein 2.1 g.

Biscuits

Servings: 6.
Time: Preparation Time: 5mins, Prepare Time: 8mins.

Ingredients

- 1 can of biscuits.

Instructions

1. Identify your rolls on to the air fryer plate.
2. Set the temperature level to 360 air-fryer for 5 minutes.
3. Turn them midway, so you obtain a positive brilliant dark tinted over the entire scone.

Nutrition Details: Calories 146.4 g, Fat 7.8 g, Carbs 17g, Sugars 5.9 g, Protein 2g.

Fruit Crumble

Servings: 2
Time: Prep Time: 5mins, Prepare Time: 12mins

Ingredients

- 1 - medium apple carefully diced
- 1/2 - cup icy blueberries strawberries, or peaches
- 1/4 - mug plus 1 tablespoon brown rice flour
- 2 - tbsps sugar
- 1/2 - tsp ground cinnamon
- 2 - tbsps nondairy
- butter.

Instructions

1. Solidify the apple as well as set blueberries in an air fryer.
2. In a little bowl, solidify the flour, sugar, cinnamon, and also unfurl.
3. Spoon the flour mix over the natural product.
4. Sprinkle a number of extra flours over the whole to cover any uncovered natural thing.
5. Cook at 350 ° F for 15 mins.
Nourishment Details: Calories 310g, Fat 12g, Carbs 50g, Sugar 26g, Healthy Protein 2g.

Puffed Egg Tarts

Servings: 3.
Time: Preparation Time: 30mins, Cook Time: 25mins.

Ingredients

- All-purpose flour.
- 1 - sheet frozen puff pastry.
- 3/4 - mug shredded cheese.
- 4 - big eggs.
- 1 - tablespoon diced fresh parsley.

Instructions

1. On a delicately floured surface, unfurl cake sheet. Cut right into 4 squares.
2. Spot 2 squares in air fryer container, dividing them separated. Air-broil for 10 mins or up until baked excellent is light fantastic darker.
3. Open up bin and also, utilizing a steel spoon, push down the concentrates of each square to make a space.
4. Sprinkle 3 tbsp cheddar right into every room and also cautiously break an egg into the centerpiece of every baked excellent.
5. Air-sear for 7 to 11 minutes or up until eggs is prepared to desired doneness.
6. Exchange to a cake rack set over waxed paper and let cool down for 5 mins. Sprinkle with a big part of the parsley, whenever wanted.
7. Rehash stages 2 to 4 with the rest of the cake squares, cheddar, eggs, and also parsley.
Nourishment Information: Calories 247g, Fat 13g, Carbs 18.2 g, Sugar 5.1 g, Protein 12.3 g.

Cinnamon Coated Donuts

Servings: 6.
Time: Prep Time: 2mins, Cook Time: 5mins.

Ingredients

- 1 - can flaky pre-made biscuit dough.
- 1/2 - mug white sugar.
- 1 - teaspoon cinnamon.
- 1/2 - mug powdered sugar.
- coconut oil.
- thawed butter.

Instructions

1. Separated and also location rolls on a minimizing board or degree surface area.
2. Use a bun shaper to lower openings amidst bread rolls.
3. Bath your air fryer crate with a hint of cooking oil, as an instance, coconut oil.
4. Area several doughnuts substantive all rounded fryer at any provided minute, guaranteeing they aren't speaking to.
5. Outdoors fryer, brush doughnuts with a little dissolved unravel and move them in either the powdered sugar.
6. Maximize your five-minute doughnuts. Nourishment Information: Calories 238g, Fat 4g, Carbs 46g, Sugars 22g, Healthy Protein 5g Air.

Blueberry Bagels

Servings: 4.
Time: Prep Time: 10mins, Prepare Time: 25mins.

Ingredients

- 1 - cup all function flour.
- 2 - tsp baking powder.
- 1/4 - tsp sea salt.
- 3-4 - packets sugar.
- 1 - cup Fage Greek yogurt.
- 1/4 - mug fresh blueberries.
- 1 - egg white.
- 2 - tsp. water.

Instructions

1. Pre-heat the air fryer to 330 degrees.

2. In a little dish sign up with the flour, heating powder, salt, as well as sugar.
3. In a medium bowl mix with each other the Greek yogurt and also blueberries.
4. Overlap the flour blend into the yogurt blend up until each of the mendings are joined.
5. Exchange the mix on to a softly floured surface and ply the batter a couple of times, breaking down the sides in a couple of times, till it is never ever again sticky.
6. Cut the butter right into 4 pieces and also fold each item right into an 8-inch-long rope.
7. Bring the two surfaces of every blend rope together to make a circle and squeeze them with each other.
8. In a little dish, whisk with each other egg white and water.
9. Brush every bagel with the egg white-water mix.
10. Consist of bagels two at a time to the air fryer and prepare for 12 minutes.
11. Get rid of and rehash process for exceptional bagels.
12. Permit to cool down on a preparing shelf or value while warm.
13. Home heating Instructions:.
14. Preheat broiler at 350 levels.
15. Area every one of the 4 bagels on a treat sheet canvassed in product paper and get ready for 25 mins.
16. Eliminate from the griddle as well as allow to cool somewhat before trading them to an air conditioning shelf.
17. Shop the cooled down bagels in an impenetrable holder or pack for as lengthy as 7 days. Or on the various other hand, strengthen the bagels in a singular layer for as lengthy as 3 months.

Nourishment Information: Calories 144g, Fat 6.05 g, Carbs 19.87 g, Sugars 2.92 g, Healthy protein 2.8 g.

Sunrise Meal Bombs

Serving: 2.
Time: Prep Time: 15mins, Cook Time: 25mins.

Ingredients
- 3 - center-cut bacon slices.
- 3 - huge eggs.
- 1/3 - less-fat cream cheese.
- 1 - tbsp fresh chives.
- 4 - ounces fresh whole-wheat pizza dough.

Instructions
1. Include eggs to bacon drippings within the area; prepare dinner, mixing frequently until nearly established yet at the identical time complimentary, rounded 1 minute.
2. Exchange eggs to a bowl; combination in cream cheddar, chives, and broke down bacon.
3. Splitting up combination right into 4 breaks in spite of pieces.
4. Roll every piece on a daintily floured surface area into a 5-inch circle.
5. Area quarter of egg blend in the consciousness of each batter circle.
6. Brush outside side of batter with water; fold combination over egg blend to mount a bag, squeezing together batter on the creases.
7. Place accumulation pouches in a single layer in air fryer bin; layer well with a cooking sprinkle.
8. Cook at 350 ° F till remarkable darker, five to 6mins, inspecting following 4mins.

Nutritional Info: Calories 305g, Fat 15g, Sugar 1g, Protein 19g.

Morning meal Pockets

Servings: 4
Time: Preparation Time: 15mins, Prepare Time: 25mins

Ingredients
1 - box smoke bread sheets
5 - eggs
1/2 - mug sausage falls apart, prepared
1/2 - mug bacon, prepared
1/2 - mug cheddar cheese, shredded

Instructions
1. Prepare eggs as basic deep-fried eggs. Include meat to the egg mix while you prepare, whenever desired.
2. Expand smoke baked excellent sheets on a getting rid of board as well as cut square forms with an intermediary or blade, guaranteeing they get on the entire attire so they will certainly fit happily with each other.
3. Spoon preferred egg, meat, and also cheddar combinations onto fifty percent of the cake square forms.
4. Identify a cake square form over the mix and also push sides along with a fork to seal.
5. Shower with sprinkle oil on the occasion that you desired a shiny, smooth baked great, nonetheless, it absolutely is optional.
6. Place morning meal pockets visible all over fryer bushel and also chefs for 8-10 mins at 370 levels.
7. Enjoy carefully as well as inspect each 2-3 mins for desired done-ness.

Nourishment Details: Calories 163g, Fat 14.25 g, Carbs 3.47 g, Sugars 1.27 g, Healthy protein 5.96 g.

Chocolate Fudge Brownies

Offering: 4.

Time: Preparation Time: 12mins, Prepare
Time: 22mins.

ACTIVE INGREDIENTS

1/2 - mug of dissolved butter.
1 - mug of sugar.
1 - tsp of vanilla remove.
2 - eggs.
1/2 - mug of flour.
1/3 - mug of cacao powder.
1 - tsp of cooking powder.

GUIDELINES.

1. Pre-heat your Air Fryer to 350 rates.
2. At that variable using non-stick food preparation sprinkle, wash your home heating frying pan.
3. In your mixing dish, integrate the liquified margarine as well as sugar.
4. Mix till light as well as feathery. Then include your eggs, vanilla, flour, cacao and also home heating powder.
5. Take into the Air fryer recipe, as well as established the clock for 20 mins.
6. Complying with 20mins, confirm whether your cakes are done, if no more consist of 5 added mins the Air Fryer.
7. Allow cool prior to offering and also.
8. Value.
Nourishment Info: Calories 61g, Fat 3g, Carbs 3g, Sugar 1g, Healthy Protein 4g.

Cauliflower Hashbrowns

Offering: 8.
Time: Preparation Time: 35mins, Prepare
Time: 1hr 20mins.

ACTIVE INGREDIENTS.

4 - pieces thick-cut bacon, diced.
1 - head of cauliflower.
1/2 - mug carefully diced onion.
1/2 - mug carefully diced red as well as environment-friendly bell pepper.
1 - egg.
1/2 - mug chickpea, almond, or all-round flour.
1 - mug grated Cheddar cheese.
1/2 - tsp paprika.
1 - tsp salt.
newly ground black pepper.

DIRECTIONS

1.Pre-heat the air fryer to 400 ° F. 2.Air-broil the bacon as well as onion for 8 to 10 mins, till the bacon is strong, drinking the shrubs a number of times amidst the food preparation treatment.
3. Fit together the head of cauliflower with a dog crate grater or carefully hack it in a nourishment cpu. You should certainly have regarding 3 1/2 cups.
4. Detect the cauliflower in the centerpiece of a best kitchen area towel and also wind it to squash all the water out.
5. Detect the cauliflower in a substantial dish and also consist of the bacon, onions, peppers, egg, flour, cheddar, paprika, salt, as well as pepper.
6. Mix till significantly signed up with. Forming the mix right into 8 oval developed patties and also pick up something like 60 mins.
7.Pre-heat air fryer to 400 ° F.
8. A shower or clean the air fryer container with a little oil. Air-broil the hash tans in globs for 10 mins, transforming them over partly via the food preparation treatment. Period with salt and also normally ground dark pepper.

Nourishment Info: Calories 146.4 g, Fat 7.8 g, Carbs 17g, Sugars 5.9 g, Healthy protein 2g.

Bacon & Eggs

Offering: 4.
Time: Preparation Time: 10mins, Prepare Time: 20mins.

COMPONENTS
4 - Ramekins.
8 - Back Bacon.
4 - Huge Eggs.
Fresh Chives optional.
Salt & Pepper.

GUIDELINES
1. Obtain the ramekins out as well as include the bacon throughout the sides as well as base of it.
2. With the objective that it covers likewise as when you're developing a baked excellent over a crusty fruit-crammed take care of.
3. Damage an egg right into the sight of each ramekin.
4. Prepare inside the Air-fryer for 180c for 13mins.
5. Period with salt as well as pepper as well as brand-new chives as well as afterwards offer.

Nourishment Info: Calories 183g, Fat 17g, Cabs 12g, Sugar 5.2 g, Healthy protein 5g.

Scrambled Eggs

Offering: 4
Time: Preparation Time: 15mins, Prepare Time: 25mins

COMPONENTS
2 - eggs
10g - saltless butter
pepper as well as salt to tast

DIRECTIONS
1. Damage both eggs.

2. Blend them.
3. Preheat air-fryer at a hundred as well as forty phases for 5 minutes. Go down the spread within the preheated air-fryer to dissolve it.
4. Whenever arranged, turn the home heating area all round to spread out the margarine out equitably.
5. Vacant the smashed egg right into the air-fryer at a hundred as well as forty arrays for 10 minutes.
6. In the celebration that you might require unique dealings with for your eggs, as an example, mushrooms, tomatoes, cheddar, drop them in currently.
7. Open up at normal periods to blend continuously till it lastly winds up feathery as well as yellow.

Nourishment Info: Calories 212.4 g, Fat 6.2 g, Carbs 15g, Sugars 6.4 g, Healthy protein 11g

Bacon Perfect Every Time

Offering: 2
Time: Preparation Time: 5mins, Prepare Time: 10mins

ACTIVE INGREDIENTS
4 - items of thick cut bacon
2 - eggs
1 - tablespoon butter
2 - croissants cut

Bacon BARBEQUE Sauce
1/2 - mug catsup
2 - tablespoon apple cider vinegar
1 - Tablespoon molasses
1 - Tablespoon brownish sugar
1/4 - tsp mustard powder
1/4 - tsp onion powder
1/2 - Tablespoon Worcestershire sauce

1/4 - tsp fluid smoke

DIRECTIONS
1. Vital Air Fryer Francis Bacon
2. Pre-heat your Air fryer to 200 degrees C.
3. Lay your selected bacon parts level coverage in real time fryer plate.
4. Prepare for four-five mins, then, transforms the bacon.
5. Prepare for every various other four-5mins up until the ideal doneness is concerned.

Nourishment Info: Calories 157.1 g, Fat 12g, Carbs 11.4 g, Sugars 6.9 g, Healthy protein 4.3 g.

Egg Rolls

Offering: 12.
Time: Preparation Time: 15mins, Prepare Time: 35mins.

INGREDIENTS
6 - eggs.
3 - mugs iced up hash browned.
8 - strips bacon.
1 - mug shredded cheese.
12 - egg roll wrappers.
1/2 - mug catsup.
1 - tbsp warm sauce.
1/2 - mug syrup.

GUIDELINES
1. Prepare the eggs in a frying pan, and also positioned apart to cool. Dark tinted the hash tans in a few other frying pan and also allow to cool.
2. Fresh the bacon in the array or in a frying pan and also reduce right into little items.
3. To make egg actions, fill up every wrapper with a tip of every one of the filling up repairings.

4. Brush the edges of the wrapper with a touch action of water to enable it to stick.
5. Roll the egg relocates securely as well as put apart till they're completely broken down.
6. Heat a frying pan over medium-excessive cozy temperature level with rounded 3 creeps of grease.
7. Scorch the egg is offered in globs, kipping down component by means of, till initial price darker and also gleaming on the 2 elements.
8. Exchange to a plate consistent with paper towels to obtain the too much oil. Offer cozy.
9. Incorporate the catsup and also cozy sauce as well as usage as a plunging sauce or existing with syrup!

Nourishment Info: Calories 656g, Fat 39g, Carbs 57g, Sugars 33g, Healthy Protein 16g.

Turkey Bacon Dish

Servings: 8
Time: Preparation Time: 5mins, Prepare Time: 30mins

Ingredients
1 - bundle Uncured Turkey Bacon

Instructions
1. Preheat air fryer to 360F.
2. Cut turkey bacon cuts right into equivalent components and also area in air fryer container.
3. Prepare for 5 mins. Outdoors fryer and also transform the bacon over.
4. Area bushel back in air fryer and also continue food preparation for 5 extra mins or till bacon is prepared acceptable to you.

Nourishment Details: Calories 30g, Fat 1.5 g, Carbs 0.9 g, Sugar 0.5 g, Healthy protein 6g

Sausage Rolls

Offering: 4
Time: Preparation Time: 20mins, Prepare Time: 25mins

Instructions
225g - Level Flour
100g - Butter
1 - Tablespoon Olive Oil
300g - Sausage Meat
1 - Tool Egg defeated
1 - Tsp Mustard
1 - Tsp Parsley
Salt & Pepper

Guidelines
1. Begin by making your cake. Detect the flour, the flavor, as well as the spread right into a mixing dish as well as making use of the combing in approach, massage the fat right into the flour up until you have a mix that appears like bread scraps.
2. Expose the cake onto a worktop and also make a square state of cake. Using a tsp massage the mustard right into the baked great.
3. Identify the wiener meat in the within as well as comb the sides of the baked excellent with egg.
4. Go up the frankfurter folds up and also later dividers right into little bits. Brush the tops and also sides of the frankfurter relocates with even more eggs.
5. Cut the acme of the frankfurter relocates with a blade so they obtain the chance to kick back.

6. Prepare in the Air-fryer at 160c for 20 mins as well as afterwards for a more 5 mins at 200c with the objective that you can have that perfect crispy baked great.

Nourishment Details: Calories 659g, Fat 45g, Carbs 43g, Sugar 2g, Healthy Protein 18g

Vegan Beignets

Servings: 24.
Time: Preparation Time: 30mins, Prepare Time: 1hr 30mins.

Ingredients
1 - mug Sugar Cooking Blend.
1 - tsp natural corn starch.

For the proofing:.
1 - mug coconut milk.
3 - tsp powdered cooking mix.
1 1/2 - tsp energetic cooking yeast.

For the dough:.
2 - tsp thawed coconut oil.
2 - tbsps aquafaba.
2 - tsps vanilla.
3 - mugs white flour.

Directions
1. Consist Of the entire Planet Cooking Blend as well as corn starch to your blender or food processor and also mix up until great smooth.
2. The corn starch will certainly secure it from collecting so you can save it on the off opportunity that you do not use all of it in the formula.
3. Heat the coconut milk up until it's cozy nevertheless awesome sufficient that you can stick your finger in it without eating on your own.

4. Making use of the oar link, assimilate the coconut oil, Aquafina, and also vanilla.

5. Then consist of the flour a container at any kind of provided minute.

6. When the flour is assimilating as well as the mix is leaving much from the sides of the mixer, modification to your batter arrest on the off opportunity that you have one.

7. The blend will certainly be wetter than if you were making a section of bread, yet you should certainly have the capability to wipe off the batter as well as framework a sphere without it staying gazing you in the face.

8. Area combination in a dish as well as spread with a best kitchen area towel as well as allow rise for 1hr.

9. Spray some flour over a huge getting rid of board and also motion of congratulations the blend right into a square form that has to do with 1/3 inch thick.

10. Cut right into 24 squares as well as allow confirmation for thirty minutes prior to you prepare them.

11. Pre-heat your air fryer to 390 levels. Contingent upon the period of your air fryer you can place 3 to 6 beignets in at the same time.

12. Prepare for 3 mins on one side. Turn them, then prepare an extra 2 mins.

13. Because air fryers vary, you might require to prepare your own another minute or more for them to obtain fantastic darker.

14. Sprinkle kindly with the powdered preparing mix you made to begin with as well as value!

15. Maintain food preparation in collections till they are completely prepared.

16. Pre-heat your griddle to 350 levels.

17. Sprinkle kindly with the powdered preparing mix you made prior to all else as well as value.

Nourishment Details: Calories 1254g, Fat 66g, Carbs 130g, Sugars 49g, Healthy Protein 35g.

Morning Meal Sausage Surprise

Offering: 8.
Time: Preparation Time: 5mins, Prepare Time: 10mins.

COMPONENTS

2 - Parts American Cheese reduced right into 1/4's.
1 - Can of 8 matter Refrigerated Crescent Roll Dough.
8 - Wood Skewers.
Syrup, Catsup or BARBEQUE for dipping.

DIRECTIONS

1. On a degree surface area, different Crescent Rolls.
2. Open up Sausages.
3. Cut Cheese.
4. Place One Crescent Roll ostensibly, unrolled.
5. Job from Wide Triangular to the pointer of the triangular.
6. Include frankfurter and also cheddar strip to the best item of the bow roller.
7. Pressure each end over frankfurter as well as cheddar.
8. Roll as well as put the rest of the blend up until you attain the pointer of the triangular.
9. Attempt to press all the batter.
10. Identify approximately 4 of these in Air Fryer.
11. Select 380 ° for 3 mins.
12. Leave as well as consist of stick.
13. Plate as well as existing with BARBEQUE, Catsup or Syrup for soaking.

Nourishment Info: Calories 226g, Fat 2g, Cabs 37g, Sugar 2g, Healthy Protein 3g.

Air Fried Sandwich

Preparation time: 10 mins
Cooking time: 6 minutes
Servings: 2

Components:
- 2 English muffins, cut in half
- 2 eggs
- 2 bacon strips
- Salt as well as black pepper to the preference

Instructions:
1. Crack eggs in your air fryer, add bacon on top, cover and also cook at 392 levels F for 6 mins.
2. Heat up your English muffin halves in your microwave for a few seconds, divide rally 2 halves, include bacon ahead, period with salt and pepper, cover with the various other 2 English muffins and also serve for breakfast.
Take pleasure in!

Nourishment: calories 261, fat 5, fiber 8, carbohydrates 12, healthy protein 4

Lunch

Chick-fil-A Chicken Sandwich

Servings: 6
Time: Preparation Time: 10mins, Prepare Time: 16mins

Ingredients
2 - Poultry Breasts Boneless/Skinless battered
1/2 - mug Dill Pickle Juice
2 - Eggs
1/2 - mug Milk
1 - mug All Objective Flour
2 - Tablespoons Powdered Sugar
2 - Tablespoons Potato Starch
1 - tsp Paprika
1 - tsp Sea Salt
1/2 - tsp Ground Black Pepper
1/2 - tsp Garlic Powder
1/4 - tsp Ground Celery Seed ground
1 - Tbsp Additional Virgin Olive Oil
1 - Oil Mister
4 - Burger Buns toasted
8 - Dill Pickle Chips
Spicy Choice
1/4 - tsp Chili pepper

DIRECTIONS
1. Find hen right into a Ziploc Baggie and also extra pound, with the goal that the full item is a comparable density, around 1/2 inch thick.

2. Place little bits of poultry once again right into Ziploc baggie and also gather pickle juice. Marinade within the colder for someplace around a half-hour.
3. In one more dish, combine flour, starch, as well as all tastes.
4. Get rid of too much flour.
5. Bath the dog crate of your air fryer with Oil as well as notification chook right into air fryer and also sprinkle the poultry with oil.
6. Prepare at 340 degrees for 6 mins. Making use of silicone tongs, very carefully transform the poultry as well as sprinkle with oil.
7. Elevate the temperature level to 4 hundred rates and also chef supper for 2 mins on each aspect.
8. Offer on buttered and also toasted buns, with 2 pickle chips and also a touch bit of mayo, on every celebration preferred.

Nourishment Info: Calories 281g, Fat 6g, Carbs 38g, Sugar 5g, Healthy Protein 15g

Pollo Quesadilla

Servings: 4
Time: Preparation Time: 15mins, Prepare Time: 10mins

COMPONENTS

Soft Taco Shells
Poultry Fajita Strips
1/2 - mug cut environment-friendly peppers
1/2 - mug cut onions
Shredded Mexican Cheese
Salsa
Sour cream

DIRECTIONS

1. Preheat Air Fryer on 370 levels for around 3 mins.
2. Shower frying pan naturally with grease.
3. Place 1 fragile taco covering in frying pan.
4. Area ruined cheddar on the covering.
5. Expand fajita hen fingers so they remain in a singular layer.
6. Place your onions as well as eco-friendly peppers over your hen.
7. Consist of progressively ruined cheddar.
8. Place an additional fragile taco covering ahead as well as shower gently with grease.
9. Establish clock for 4 mins.
10. Turn over very carefully with a huge spatula.
11. Shower gently with grease and also place shelf over the covering to hold it establish.
12. Establish clock for 4 mins.
13. On the off possibility that it's not solid sufficient for you, leave in for a number of added mins.
14. Get rid of as well as reduce right into 4 cuts or 6 cuts.
15. Existing with Salsa as well as acrid lotion whenever desired.

Nourishment Info: Calories 370.3 g, Fat 10.2 g, Carbs 54g, Sugars 2.3 g, Healthy protein 20.7 g.

Hotdogs

Servings: 2.
Time: Preparation Time: 5mins, Prepare Time: 10mins.

COMPONENTS

2 - hotdogs.
2 - hotdog buns.
2 - tbsps grated cheese if preferred.

DIRECTIONS

1. Detect 2 wieners right into the air fryer, prepare yourself dinner for cycle 5mins.
2. Discover the wiener on a bun, along with cheddar on each occasion required.
3. Place clothed wiener right into the air fryer, as well as chef for an additionally 2 mins.
Nourishment Details: Calories 289g, Fat 13g, Carbs 29g, Sugars 2g, Healthy Protein 12g.

Quick Pita Bread Cheese Pizza.

Offering: 3.
Time: Preparation Time: 10mins, Prepare Time: 10mins.

COMPONENTS

1 - Pita Bread.
1 - Tbsp Pizza Sauce.
1/4 - mug Mozarella Cheese.
1 - drizzle Additional Virgin Olive Oil.
1 - Stainless-steel Short Legged Trivet.

Toppings:

7 - pieces Pepperoni or even more.
1/4 - mug Sausage.
1 - Tbsp Yellow/Brown Onion cut slim.
1/2 - tsp Fresh Garlic diced.

DIRECTIONS

1. Make use of a spoon as well as twirl Pizza Sauce on Pita Bread. Include your most liked correctings as well as Cheese.
2. Consist of a little spray of Additional Virgin Olive Oil over top of Pizza.
3. Place in Air Fryer and also detect a Trivet over Pita Bread. Prepare at 350 levels for 6 mins.
4. Meticulously remove from Air Fryer as well as cut.

Nourishment Details: Calories 239.4 g, Fat 2g, Carbs 42.7 g, Sugars 2.7 g, Healthy protein 15.2 g.

Grilled American Cheese

Servings: 2.
Time: Preparation Time: 5mins, Prepare Time: 10mins.

COMPONENTS

2 - pieces Sandwich Bread.
2-3 - pieces Cheddar Cheese.
2 - tsps Butter or Mayo.

DIRECTIONS

1. Place cheddar in between bread cuts as well as spread out the beyond both cuts of bread.
2. Area in air fryer as well as chef at 370 levels for 8 mins. Flip, component of the method with.

Nourishment Info: Calories 429g, Fat 28g, Carbs 25g, Sugar 2g, Healthy Protein 18g.

Bourbon Bacon Hamburger

Servings: 2.

Time: Preparation Time: 25mins, Prepare Time: 35mins.

ACTIVE INGREDIENTS

1 - tbsp bourbon.
2 - tbsps brownish sugar.
3 - strips maple bacon.
3/4 - extra pound hamburger.
1 - tbsp diced onion.
2 - tbsps BARBEQUE sauce.
1/2 - tsp salt.
fresh ground black pepper.
2 - pieces Colby Jack cheese.
2 - Kaiser rolls.
lettuce as well as tomato.

Zesty Hamburger Sauce:

2 - tbsps BARBEQUE sauce.
2 - tbsps mayo.
1/4 - tsp ground paprika.
fresh ground black pepper.

DIRECTIONS

1. Pre-heat the air fryer to 390ºF and also clear a little water right into the base of the air fryer cupboard.
2. Settle the scotch as well as dark tinted sugar in a little dish. Detect the bacon strips obvious all over fryer container and also brush with the darker sugar mix.
3. Air-sear at 390ºF for 4 mins.
4. Settle the ground meat, onion, BARBEQUE sauce, salt and also pepper in a significant dish.
5. Exchange the hamburger patties to the air fryer dog crate and also air-broil the hamburgers at 370ºF for 15 to 20 mins, section upon exactly how you like your hamburger prepared.
6. Turn the hamburgers over component of the method with the food preparation treatment.

7. While the hamburgers are air-fricasseeing, make the hamburger sauce by settling the BARBEQUE sauce, mayo, paprika, as well as ground dark pepper to taste in a dish.

8. At the factor when the hamburgers are prepared to your favoring, leading every patty with a cut of Colby Jack cheddar and also air-sear for an added minute, simply to soften the cheddar.

9. Spread out the sauce within the Kaiser relocations, position the hamburgers on the relocations, leading with the bourbon bacon, lettuce, and also tomato as well as value!

Nourishment Details: Calories 1060g, Fat 65g, Carbs 77g, Sugars 30g, Healthy Protein 45g.

Burgers

Offering: 4
Time: Prep Time: 10mins, Cook Time: 10mins

ACTIVE INGREDIENTS

1 - Tbsp Worcestershire sauce
1 - teaspoon Maggi flavoring sauce
fluid smoke
1/2 - tsp garlic powder
1/2 - teaspoon onion powder
1/2 - teaspoon salt
1/2 - tsp ground black pepper
1 - tsp parsley
500g - ground beef

INSTRUCTIONS

1. Bath the higher Actifry plate; positioned apart. On the occasion that you are utilizing a bin kind fryer, no compelling cause to spray the bushel.

2. In bushel kinds, your cooking temperature can be one hundred eighty C/350 F.

3. In a bit dish, incorporate all the flavoring points, from the Worcestershire sauce right to as well as along with the dried parsley.

4. Add this to the burger in a large dish.

5. Blend perfectly, nonetheless, make note so as currently not to wear down the meat as that turns on extreme burgers.

6. Void the hamburger mixture into four, and also form the patties.

7. With your thumb, put an indent within the prime focus of all and also miscellaneous to preserve the patties gathering up in the center.

8. Area plate in Actifry; wash acmes of patties gently.

9. Cook 10mins for medium. There is no engaging reason to reveal the patties.

10. Offer hot on a bun with facet recipes of your choice.

Nourishment Details: Cal 148g, Fat 4g, Carbs 8g, Sugar 2.4 g, Healthy protein 24g

Roast Chicken

Serving: 2
Time: Preparation Time: 25mins, Cook Time: 55mins

INGREDIENTS

4.25 - pound entire poultry
spices

DIRECTIONS

1. Tidy poultry and also rub completely dry.

2. Sprinkle liberally with a completely dry rub or possess flavorings.

3. Dash sear bin with food preparation shower as well as spot poultry into the bushel with the legs overlooking.

4. Cook poultry for 330 levels Fahrenheit for thirty minutes.

5. Flip chicken.

6. Cook for 20 additional mins at 330 levels Fahrenheit or until internal temperature of the hen is 165 degrees Fahrenheit.

Nourishment Information: Calories 226.7 g, Fat 10.7 g, Carbs 14.2 g, Sugars 4.6 g, Healthy protein 19.2 g.

Chick fil A Chicken Nuggets

Servings: 6.
Time: Prep Time: 15mins, Prepare Time: 10mins.

Ingredients

1 - mug dill pickle juice.
1 - lb boneless skinless poultry busts.
1 - egg.
1 - mug milk.
1 1/2 - mugs flour.
3 - tablespoon powdered sugar.
2 - tsp salt.
1 1/2 - tsp pepper.
1/2 - tsp paprika.
Olive oil spritz.
Obtain Ingredients Powered by Chicory.

DIRECTIONS

1. Add poultry pieces to pickle capture and also marinade in the refrigerator for around thirty minutes.
2. Whisk milk and also egg together and also put aside.
3. Join the completely dry correctings as well as blend deposit.
4. Preheat air fryer to 370.
5. Remove the chicken from refrigerator, network and place each into the completely dry mix, to the liquid blend as well as back to the completely dry ensuring it is all around covered, emphasizing to get rid of an excess.

6. Cook in a solitary layer of hen for 8 mins or till fantastic dark tinted, turning and also spritzing with olive oil at the midway imprint.
7. Present with your most enjoyed diving sauce.

Nourishment Details: Calories 256g, Fat 5g, Carbs, 29g, Sugar 9g, Healthy Protein 22g.

Turkey & Cheese Calzone

Servings: 2.
Time: Prep Time: 10mins, Cook Time: 10mins.

Ingredients

4 - Tablespoon Homemade Tomato Sauce.
Extra Turkey brown meat shredded.
100g - Cheddar Cheese.
25g - Mozzarella Cheese grated.
25g - Back Bacon diced.
1 - Big Egg beaten.
1 - Tbsp Tomato Puree.
1 - Tsp Oregano.
1 - Tsp Basil.
1 - Tsp Thyme.
Salt & Pepper.
Metric - Imperial.

Instructions

1. Pre-heat your Air Fryer to 180c.
2. Begin by disclosing your pizza batter with the goal that they are the level of little pizzas.
3. In a little combining dish include every one of the spices equally as the tomato sauce and puree.
4. Making use of a food preparation brush include a layer of tomato sauce to your pizza bases ensuring that it does not truly get in touch with the side with a 1cm space.

5. Layer up your pizza with your turkey, bacon, as well as cheddar to the opposite.

6. With the 1cm opening around your pizza base and using your cooking brush again, brush with beaten egg.

7. Overlay your pizza base over so it takes after a raw Cornish pale and all-region that is currently noticeable of the pizza mix to be combed with more egg.

8. An area airborne Fryer for 10 minutes at 180c.

9. Offer.

Nourishment Information: Calories 158g, Fat 11g, Carbs 2g, Sugars 1g, Protein 10g.

Fried Chicken Tenders

Serving: 2.
Time: Prep Time: 10mins, Cook Time: 10mins.

Ingredients

12-- oz. of Chicken Breasts.
1 - Egg White.
1/8 - Mug Flour.
35g - Panko Bread Crumbs.
Salt and also Pepper.

Instructions

1. Cut poultry bosom of any too much fat as well as cut into tenders. Period each side with salt and pepper.

2. Plunge poultry fingers right into flour, then egg whites, at that point panko bread morsels.

3. Worry right into air fryer container and also shower with olive splash.

4. Prepare at 350 degrees for around 10 minutes or till prepared via.

Nourishment Info: Calories 293g, Fat 4g, Carbs 53g, Sugar 7g, Protein 9g.

Banana Sandwich

Servings: 2
Time: Preparation Time: 10mins, Cook Time: 10mins

Ingredients

butter, softened
4 - slices white bread
1/4 - mug chocolate hazelnut spread
1 - banana

Instructions

1. Pre-heat the air fryer to 370°F.

2. Spread the mellowed margarine on one side of the substantial variety of cuts of bread and also place the cuts, buttered side down on the counter. Spread the delicious chocolate hazelnut spread on the opposite side of the bread cuts. Cut the banana down the middle as well as afterward reduce every fifty percent into three cuts the lengthy method. Detect the banana cuts on 2 cuts of bread and top with the rest of the cuts of bread to make 2 sandwiches. Cut the sandwiches down the middle (triangles or square shapes)-- this will help them all fit visible all over fryer without a moment's delay. Exchange the sandwiches to the air fryer.

3. Air-broil at 370°F for 5 minutes. Flip the sandwiches over as well as air-broil for another 2 to 3 mins or till the leading bread cuts are pleasantly cooked. Existing yourself with a glass of milk or a midnight nightcap while the sandwiches cool down marginally and also appreciate

Chicken Fried Rice

Servings: 2.
Time: Prep Time: 20mins, Prepare Time: 40mins.

Ingredients

3 - mugs cooked white rice cold.
1 - cup cooked chicken diced.
1 - cup icy peas and carrots.
6 - tbsp soy sauce.
1 - tablespoon grease.
1/2 - cup onion diced.

Instructions

1. Spot prepared white rice into the mixing dish.
2. Include the grease as well as the soy sauce as well as mix completely.
3. Include the solidified peas and carrots, the diced onion and the diced hen and also blend entirely.
4. Vacant the rice mix right into the nonstick dish.
5. Detect the dish right into the Air Fryer.
6. Establish the Air Fryer to 360 f with a 20 minute cooking time.
7. When the clock goes off, get rid of the dish from the Air Fryer.
8. Existing with your most enjoyed meat, or just get a bowl as well as value.

Fried Chicken

Serving: 4.
Time: Prep Time: 10mins, Prepare Time: 25mins.

Ingredients

1/2 - cup all objective flour.
1 - egg defeated.
4 - small poultry thighs skin on.
1 1/2 - tablespoon Old Bay Cajun Spices.
1 - tsp seasoning salt.
cooking spray if desired.

Instructions

1.Pre-warmth the Air Fryer to 390 degrees.
2. Blend jointly the flour, salt, and also the Old Bay.
3. Dig the chicken thru the flour mix, at that aspect into the egg, at that element over once again into the flour combo again.
4. Get rid of oversupply flour high-quality.
5. On the off threat which you need to, you may bath the chook with cooking splash delicately currently, but I don't difficulty.
6. Identify the four chook thighs into the base of the Air-fryer cooking area.
7. Prepare for 25mins or till the poultry achieves a hundred and eighty levels.
8. Expel as well as offer.

Rotisserie Whole Chicken

Servings: 4
Time: Prep Time: 15mins, Cook Time: 1hr 5mins.

Ingredients

1 - Whole Poultry cleaned up and also blotted completely dry.
2 - Tablespoons Ghee.
1 - Tablespoon TOG House Flavoring.

Instructions

1. Eliminate giblet package deal from hen and also pat completely dry.
2. Massage Ghee/Oil throughout hen and period liberally.
3. Detect chicken, breast element down right into Air Fryer.
4. Prepare at 350 levels for half-hour.
5. Turn chook over and cook for 350 levels for an additional half-hour.
6. Let rest for 10mins and also afterwards offer.

Chinese Sweet' N Sour Pork

Servings: 4.
Time: Preparation Time: 15mins, Prepare Time: 12mins.

Ingredients

2 - extra pounds Pork cut into portions.
2 - huge Eggs.
1 - teaspoon Pure Sesame Oil.
1 - cup Potato Starch.
1/2 - tsp Sea Salt.
1/4 - teaspoon Newly Ground Black Pepper.
1/16 - teaspoon Chinese 5 Seasoning.
3 - Tablespoons Canola Oil.

Various other Ingredients

Oil Mister.

Instructions

1. In one mixing dish, combine the potato starch, salt, pepper, and Chinese Five Seasoning.
2. In one more mixing bowl, defeated the eggs and also include Sesame Oil.
3. Dig the pork items into the Potato Starch as well as shake off any kind of surplus.
4. Quickly plunge each piece right into the egg blend, get rid of surplus as well as after that again into the Potato Starch mix.
5. Layer Air Fryer Basket with oil. Spot pork pieces into bin and also sprinkle with oil.
6. Cook at 340 degrees for around 8-12 mins, drinking the pet crate 2 or multiple times.
7. Existing with my Easy Wonderful 'N Sour Sauce Dish.

Chicken Parmesan

Serving: 4.
Time: Prep Time: 25mins, Cook Time: 20mins.

Ingredients

- 8 - oz each chicken bust.
- 6 - tablespoon experienced breadcrumbs.
- 2 - tbsp grated Parmesan cheese.
- 1 - tablespoon butter.
- 6 - tbsp reduced fat mozzarella cheese.
- 1/2 - mug marinara.

cooking spray.

Instructions

1. Bath the lolled naturally with a splash.
2. Sign up with breadcrumbs as well as parmesan cheddar in a bowl.
3. Liquify the unfold in any kind of other bowl.
4. Carefully comb the spread onto the poultry, then dunk into breadcrumb combo.
5. At the factor whilst the air fryer is prepared, region 2 portions within the bin and also splash the top with oil.
6. Cook 6mins, flip and also pinnacle each with 1 tablespoon sauce and also half tbsp of ruined mozzarella cheddar.
7. Prepare three additional minutes or till cheddar is softened.
8. Put apart and hold warm, rehash with the remainder of the 2 portions.

Lemon Pepper Chicken

Serving: 1
Time: Prep Time: 5mins, Cook Time: 15mins

Ingredients

- 1 - Chicken Bust
- 2 - Lemons skin and juice
- 1 - Tablespoon Poultry Spices
- 1 - Tsp Garlic Puree
- Handful Black Peppercorns
- Salt & Pepper

Instructions

1. Pre-heat the air fryer to 180c.

2. Establish your job station. Identify a large sheet of silver aluminum foil on the worktop and add to it each of the seasonings and also the lemon skin.

3. Spread out your poultry breasts onto a reducing board and trim off any greasy bits or any type of little bones that are still there.

4. Then season each side with salt as well as pepper. Scrub the hen flavor into the two sides with the objective that it is partially an alternate shading.

5. Find it in the silver aluminum foil sheet and also massage it well with the objective that it is completely prepared.

6. At that point seal it up exceptionally limited with the goal that it can not inhale as this will aid get the flavor right into it.

7. Then provide it a slap with a moving pin so it will certainly smooth it out as well as release more taste.

8. Detect it visible all over fryer for 15 minutes as well as verify whether it is entirely cooked in the center before offering.

Nashville Hot Chicken

Servings: 4
Time: Prep Time: 22mins, Prepare Time: 35mins

Ingredients
- 1 - hen
- 2 - eggs
- 1 - mug buttermilk
- 2 - cups versatile flour
- 2 - tablespoons paprika
- 1 - tsp garlic powder
- 1 - tsp onion powder
- 2 - tsps salt
- 1 - tsp black pepper
- Grease

Nashville Hot Sauce:
- 1 - tablespoon chili pepper

- 1 - tsp salt
- 1/4 - mug vegetable oil
- 4 - slices white bread
- dill pickle pieces

Instructions
1. Cut the chicken bosoms right into 2 pieces so you have a sum of 8 littles hen.

2. Set up a two-arrange excavating terminal.

3. Sign up with the flour, paprika, garlic powder, onion powder, salt, and dark pepper in a zipper-sealable plastic sack.

4. Dunk the chicken items right into the egg-buttermilk mix; then toss them in the ready flour, covering all sides.

5. Pre-heat the air fryer to 370°F. Sprinkle or clean the base of the air-fryer bushel with a little vegetable oil.

6. Air-broil the poultry in 2 lots at 370°F for 20 mins, turning the pieces over partly through the cooking procedure.

7. Exchange the poultry to a plate, nonetheless, doesn't cover.

8. Lower the temperature level coverage in genuine time fryer to 340 ° F. 9. Flip the poultry back completed and also position the main clump of poultry over the second cluster as of now in the crate.

10. Air-broil for an added 7 mins.

11. While the poultry is air-browning, settle the chili pepper and also salt in a bowl.

12. Warmth the vegetable oil in a little pot and also when it is extremely warm, add it to the flavor blend.

13. Identify the seared chicken over the white bread cuts and also brush the hot sauce around poultry.

14. Top with the pickle cuts as well as offer cozy. Appreciate the heat and the taste

---

Buttermilk Chicken

Serving: 1

Time: Prep Time: 15mins, Cook Time: 25mins

Ingredients

- 800g - chicken upper legs
- Marinade
- 2 - cups buttermilk
- 2 - teaspoons salt
- 2 - teaspoons black pepper
- 1 - teaspoon cayenne pepper
- Seasoned Flour
- 2 - mugs all function flour
- 1 - tbsp baking powder
- 1 - tbsp garlic powder
- 1 - tbsp paprika powder
- 1 - teaspoon salt

Instructions

1. Wash chicken upper legs to remove any kind of conspicuous fat and also build-up, and also pat dry with paper towels.
2. Toss together hen pieces, dark pepper, paprika and also salt in an extensive dish to layer.
3. Pour buttermilk over until hen is coated. Refrigerated for no much less than 6 hrs or medium-term.
4. Preheat air-fryer at 180 ° C.
5. In a self-governing dish, integrate flour, preparing powder, paprika as well as salt, and pepper.
6. Eliminate the hen 1 piece simultaneously from the buttermilk and also dig in ready flour.
7. Shake off any excess flour as well as exchange to a plate.
8. Manage hen one layer on the fryer crate, skin side up, and move the container into the air-fryer.
9. Establish clock and also air sear for 8 minutes. Haul out the plate, transform hen items over, as well as established the clock for an extra 10 minutes.
10. Allow to diminish theoretically towels as well as serve.

Imitator KFC Popcorn Chicken

Serving: 12.
Time: Preparation Time: 10mins, Prepare Time: 12mins.

Ingredients

- 1 - Hen Breast.
- 2ml - KFC Spice Blend obtain the recipe right here.
- 60ml - Bread Crumbs.
- 1 - Little Egg beaten.
- 50g - Level Flour.
- Salt & Pepper.
- Metric - Imperial.

Instructions

1. In the food, processor blend your hen until it takes after minced chicken.
2. Establish a handling plant line with a bowl with your flour and also a 2nd bowl with your ruined egg.
3. In a third bowl combine your KFC flavor mix, your salt as well as pepper and later your bread pieces.
4. At that point like a commercial facility, line up make your minced poultry right into balls and come in the flour, the egg as well as later the spiced bread scraps.
5. Spot noticeable around fryer at 180c for 10-12 mins or till prepared in the facility.

Chicken Tikkas

Servings: 2.
Time: Prep Time: 25mins, Prepare Time: 1hr 10mins.

Ingredients

For marinade:.

- Boneless Poultry-- 500gms.
- Thick yoghurt-- 200gms.
- 3 - Bell peppers.
- Cherry Tomatoes-- 100gms.
- Fresh ginger garlic paste-- 1 -tbsp.
- Red Chilli Powder-- 2 tablespoon.
- Turmeric Powder-- 1 tsp.
- Coriander Powder-- 2 tablespoon.
- Cumin Powder-- 2 tablespoon.
- Olive oil-- 2 tsp.
- Salt to taste.

For Garnishing:
- Fresh Coriander-- 1/3 cup.
- Fresh Mint Leaves-- couple of.
- 1 - Onion.
- 1 - Lemon.

Instructions
1. In a large dish, integrate every one of the correctings under marinate and also coat the hen well with tastes.
2. Spread and allow it sit for 2 hrs. On the occasion that possible, medium-term.
3. Request that your youngsters help you in stringing the hen, tomatoes, and also peppers then again on the sticks and also keep them prepared.
4. Preheat Philips Air Fryer for 5 mins at 200 Degrees C.
5. Line the bin with light weight aluminum foil and area the sticks.
6. Flame broil for 12-15 minutes, transforming each stick once in the center of so it cooks equitably.
7. Evacuate in a plate. Trimming with coriander, mint, onions and squash a lime prior to offering.

Flourless Chicken Cordon Bleu

Serving: 2.
Time: Preparation Time: 15mins, Cook Time: 30mins.

Ingredients
- 2 - Chicken Breasts.
- 1 - Cut Cheddar Cheese.
- 1 - Tbsp Soft Cheese.
- 1 - Cut Pork.
- 20g - Oats.
- 1 - Tiny Egg defeated.
- 1 - Tsp Garlic Puree.
- 1 - Tsp Parsley.
- 1 - Tbsp Tarragon.
- 1 - Tablespoon Thyme.
- Salt & Pepper.
- Metric - Imperial.

Instructions
1. Preheat your air fryer to 180c.
2. On a cleaving tons up place your poultry bosoms.
3. Cleave them at a side edge to straight near to the edge so you can overlay them over as well as include mendings to the middle.
4. In a blending, dish includes the delicate cheddar, garlic, and parsley and also blend well.
5. Identify a layer of the cheddar blend in the center along with 1/2 a cut each of the cheddar and the pork.
6. Push down on the poultry so presumably that it is taken care of with a layer of loading inside it.
7. In one dish includes the egg and in one more consist of the blended oats.
8. In the blended oats bowl furthermore, consist of the thyme as well as mix well.
9. Roll the hen in the oats first, then the egg as well as back in the oats.
10. Spot your poultry pieces on a preparing sheet in your air fryer as well as cook for 30 minutes at 180c.
11. Complying with 20 minutes transform it over with the goal that both sides obtain the possibility to be company.
12. Existing with brand-new potatoes.

Sweet Cream Cheese Wontons

Serving: 3

Time: Prep Time: 30mins, Cook Time: 15mins

Ingredients

- 8 - oz. mollified cream cheddar
- ½ - container powdered sugar
- 12 - oz. wonton wraps
- 1 - egg rushed with a sprinkle of water

To Fry:
48 - oz. canola oil

To Bake:

Nonstick Cooking Spray

Instructions

1. Blend the powdered sugar and cream cheddar together until especially joined.
2. Spread out around 4 wontons at some random minute and spread the remaining with a drying towel
3. Fill a little bowl with water and set near the wontons.
4. A spot about a ½ teaspoon of cream cheddar mix in the midst of each wonton.
5. Dunk your fingers into the whisked egg/water mix, and overlay the wontons corner to corner to outline a triangle. Seal and certification that there are no air bubbles.
6. Plunge your fingers yet again into the water. With the longest side of the triangle standing up to you, wrinkle the left side to the other side, and after that overlay the left side over it, to the other side.

7. Rehash until all wontons are filled and wrapped

Reuben Egg Rolls

Serving: 4
Time: Prep Time: 15mins, Cook Time: 10mins

Ingredients

- Egg move wrappers
- Cut Corned Beef or Pastrami
- Jar of sauerkraut
- Swiss cheddar
- Vegetable oil shower
- 1000 Island Dressing

Instructions

1. Cut Corned Beef into tight cuts. Cut Swiss cheddar into flimsy cuts.
2. Channel Sauerkraut and get dry.
3. Take 1 egg move wrapper and douse edges with water so it will seal together when you overlay it over. Point the corner towards you.
4. Stack the Corned Beef and Swiss cheddar in return layers.
5. Finish it off with a little or a lot of sauerkraut.
6. Take the coordinated end closest toward you and wrinkle over the substance.
7. Raise the sides and wrinkle in. Continue falling until no doubt an egg rolls.
8. Shower tenderly on the different sides with vegetable oil sprinkle.
9. Spot in Air Fryer Basket.
10. Air Fry at 400° for 7 minutes, flip and an extra 7 minutes on the contrary side. You can change the warming time to whether you like them light or diminish.
11. Expel with tongs from Air Fryer and present with 1000 island dressing.

Jalapeno Poppers

Serving: 4
Time: Prep Time: 15mins, Cook Time: 30mins

Ingredients

10 - jalapeno peppers
8 - oz of cream cheddar I utilized a without dairy cream cheddar
¼ - c new parsley
¾ - c without gluten tortilla or bread morsels

Instructions

1. Combine 1/2 of pieces and smooth cheddar. At the point when united incorporate the parsley.
2. Stuff each pepper with this mix.
3. Delicately press the most elevated purposes of the peppers into the remainder of the 1/4 c of scraps to make the top covering.
4. Cook in an air fryer at 370 degrees F for 6-8 minutes OR in a standard stove at 375 degrees F for 20 minutes.
5. Let cool and ENJOY

Philly Cheesesteak Egg Rolls

Serving: 4
Time: Prep Time: 35mins, Cook Time: 10mins

Ingredients

- 2 - Packages of Frozen Sliced Steak
- 1 - Package Egg Roll Wrappers
- 1 - Green Bell Pepper
- 1 - Medium White Onion
- ½ - Pound of Cheese

Instructions

1. Begin by dicing your onion. The green pepper is straightaway.
2. Same thing. Give it a fine shaker.
3. In a hot, enormous dish, with a shower of olive oil, sauté your vegetables until they are cooked yet in the meantime crips.
4. A bit of shading adds a trademark sweetness to the vegetables.
5. Expel them to a paper towel-lined plate and get ready to cook your hardened cut steak.
6. Utilize the comparable hot dish that I cooked the vegetables in.
7. The flavors left over from the onions and peppers will mix with the meat as it cooks.
8. Include a dash of salt and pepper to the meat as it cooks. This is optional and you should upgrade your meat to your taste.
9. Utilize a dimension metal spatula to part the meat up into snack assessed pieces as it cooks.
10. Give the meat an opportunity to cook until it will lose the last bit of pink.
11. In an extensive bowl, join your meat, cheddar, and cooked peppers and onions.
12. This is the reason that you need meat and veggies to cool. In case they are not cool enough the cheddar will start to mellow.
13. It isn't the end of the world if the cheddar condenses anyway it will make for more straightforward rolling if your cheddar isn't gooey!
14. On an ideal, dry surface the opportunity has arrived to climb your Philly cheddar steak egg rolls.

Party Meatballs

Serving: 24
Time: Prep Time: 20mins, Cook Time: 15mins

Ingredients

- 1 - lb Mince Beef
- ¾ - Cup Tomato Ketchup
- 1 - Tbsp Tabasco
- 2 ½ - Tbsp Worcester Sauce
- ¼ - Cup Vinegar
- 1 - Tbsp Lemon Juice
- ½ - Cup Brown Sugar
- ½ - Tsp Dry Mustard
- 3 - Gingersnaps pulverized

Instructions

1. In a wide blending bowl zone in your seasonings and blend well.
2. All together that the whole thing is reliably secured.
3. Add the mince to the bowl and mix agreeably.
4.Structure into medium evaluated meatballs and notification them into your Air Fryer.
5. Cook them for 15mins on a 190c warmth
6. Spot them on sticks sooner than serving.

Panko Breaded Chicken

Parmesan with Marinara Sauce

Serving: 4
Time: Prep Time: 10mins, Cook Time: 20mins

Ingredients

- 16 - oz skinless chicken bosoms
- 1 - glass panko bread pieces
- ½ - glass parmesan cheddar ground
- ½ - glass mozzarella cheddar destroyed
- 1/8 - glass egg whites
- ¾ - glass marinara sauce
- 2 - tsp Italian Seasoning
- salt and pepper to taste

Instructions

1. Get the equation for marinara sauce here.
2. Preheat the Air Fryer to 400. Sprinkle the holder with cooking shower.
3. Cut the chicken chests down the center equitably to make 4 progressively thin chicken chests. Detect the chicken chests on a hard surface and pound them to absolutely smooth.
4. Consolidate the panko breadcrumbs, cheddar, and seasonings in a bowl adequately sweeping to dive the chicken chests. Mix to unite.
5. Spot the egg whites in a bowl adequately sweeping to dive the chicken.
6. Plunge the chicken in the egg whites and thereafter the breadcrumbs mix.
7. Spot in the Air Fryer. Shower the most elevated purpose of the chicken with cooking sprinkle.
8. Cook for 7 minutes. Top all of the chests with marinara sauce and the obliterated mozzarella. Cook for an additional 3 minutes or until cheddar has disintegrated.

Mozzarella Sticks

Serving: 4
Time: Prep Time: 20mins, Cook Time: 2hrs 20mins

Ingredients

- 2 - Eggs
- 3 - tablespoon Milk, nonfat
- 0.25 - container Flour, white
- 1 - container bread scraps

Instructions

1. Cut cheddar into 3 x 1/2 inch sticks.

2. Spot bread pieces in a bowl. Detect our own in a bowl. Consolidate the egg and milk and put in a bowl.
3. Dunk cheddar sticks in our, by then egg, and nally bread scraps.
4. Lay breaded sticks on an at treat sheet.
5. Stop in cooler for 1-2 hours or until solid.
6. Spot little gatherings of breaded sticks (don't stuff) into the Fry Basket.
7. Press the M Button. Look to the French Fries Icon.
8. Press the Power Button and modify cooking time to 12 minutes at 400 degrees.

4. AF the wings with a hundred and eighty C for 6mins.
5. Flip over 180c for 6mins and flip yet again AF two hundred for 3mins.
6. Give it a peril to chill for 5mins, present with a wedge of lime/lemon.

Lime Chicken Wings

Serving: 4
Time: Prep Time: 45mins, Cook Time: 6hrs 40mins

Ingredients

- 16 - chicken wings

Marinate

- 2 - tbsp light soya sauce
- 2 - tbsp great quality nectar
- ½ - tsp ocean salt
- ¼ - tsp white pepper powder
- ½ - pulverize dark pepper
- 2 - tbsp lime/lemon juice

Instructions

1. Empty all marinate into a pitcher dish, comprise of mid-wings.
2. Combo pleasantly and permit it season for something close to 6 hour
3. Convey out to unwinding in room temperature for 30mins sooner than warmth.

Buffalo Cauliflower

Serving: 4
Time: Prep Time: 10mins, Prepare Time: 15mins

Ingredients
For the Cauliflower
- 4 - mugs cauliflower florets
- 1 - cup panko breadcrumbs
- For the Buffalo Coating
- 1/4 - cup melted vegan butter
- 1/4 - cup after melting
- 1/4 - cup vegan Buffalo sauce For Dipping

Instructions
1. Dissolve the veggie lover spread in a mug in the microwave, then rush in the wild ox sauce.
2. Holding by the stem, dunk every floret in the margarine/wild ox mix, obtaining most of the floret covered in sauce.
3. It's fine if a touch of the stem doesn't obtain saucy. Hold the floret over the mug up until it generally quits dribbling.

4. A number of dribbles are OKAY, however on the off opportunity that its dropping sauce, your panko will obtain clumpy and give up staying likewise.

5. Dig the soaked floret in the panko/salt blend, covering as much as you can imagine, at that point area noticeable throughout a fryer.

6. No engaging reason to stress over a solitary layer. Just drop it in there.

7. Air sear at 350F (don't preheat) for 14-17 minutes, drinking a couple of times as well as examining their innovation when you drink.

8. Your cauliflower is done when the florets are somewhat seared.

9. Existing with your plunging sauce of choice.

Buffalo Wings

Servings: 4
Time: Prep Time: 10mins, Prepare Time: 30mins

Ingredients

- 1 - pound. Hen Wings
- 1/2 - cup Frank's Hot Sauce
- Fat Free Blue Cheese

Instructions

1. Preheat air fryer for 3-5 minutes at 380 °
2. Spot poultry wings in a solitary layer in air fryer.
3. Air-fryer for 12 mins at 380 °
4. Flip wings and air-fryer for an added 12 mins
5. You can include your sauce now, or toward the finish of your cooking.
6. After the 12 minutes is done - transform the temperature level as much as 400 ° and also chef for 5 added mins.
7. See to it the inward temperature of the wings are 165 ° prior to getting rid of

8. In the event that you really did not include your sauce amid the food preparation, at that point area in a bowl as well as include your popular sauce as well as shake or toss till wings are protected.

Honey Bourbon Poultry Wings

Serving: 4
Time: Prep Time: 10mins, Cook Time: 25mins

INGREDIENTS

- 3-5 - pounds Chicken Wing
- 3/4 - cup Ketchup
- 1 - Tbsp Fluid Smoke
- 1/2 - mug Light Brown Sugar
- 1/4 - mug Yellow/Brown Onion
- 2 - cloves Fresh Garlic finely
- 1/2 - mug Fresh Water
- 1/4 - cup Bourbon
- 2 - tsps Paprika
- 1/4 - tsp Cayenne Pepper
- 3 - Tablespoons Clover Honey
- 1 - teaspoon Sea Salt
- 1/2 - tsp Ground Black Pepper

INSTRUCTIONS

1. Press the Sauté or Browning capture on your Stress Cooker.
2. Consist of catsup, liquid smoke, darker sugar, onion, and also garlic to your Stress Stove cooking pot.
3. Mix until sauce starts to enlarge, around 5 mins.
4. Consist of the water and also the remainder of the repairings.
5. Meticulously consist of the wings and blend into the sauce.
6. Lock on the leading and Shut the Stress Shutoff. Cook over Pressure for 5 mins.
7. At the point when Beep seems, complete a Quick Launch.

8. Transform the Pressure Cooker to Sauté or Browning and allow sauce to thicken while the wings are crisping in the stove.

9. Area dog crate into air fryer and set the temperature to 400 levels Fahrenheit for 6 mins.

10. Find any kind of additional sauce right into a bowl and also usage for diving.

Snacks

Bacon Cashews

Servings: 12
Time: Preparation Time: 10mins, Prepare Time: 15mins

INGREDIENTS

- 3 - cups raw cashews
- 2 - tsps salt
- 3 - tablespoons fluid smoke
- 2 - tablespoons blackstrap molasses

INSTRUCTIONS

1. In a large bowl, hurl together the majority of the mendings, making a point to coat the cashews actually well.

2. Vacant the cashews right into your air fryer bin, and cook at 350F for 8-10 mins, drinking at routine periods to guarantee they prepare equitably as well as to look for doneness.

3. Amidst the most recent 2 mins, you need to shake/check each minute to avoid consuming. The line amongst done and consumed can be slight with this formula.

4. Give them an opportunity to cool to room temperature level-- around 10-15 minutes-- at that point exchange to a water/air proof stockpiling compartment.

Potato Chips

Serving: 4
Time: Prep Time: 30mins, Cook Time: 55mins

INGREDIENTS

2 - medium sized Sugary food Potatoes
1/4 - mug of Olive Oil
1 - tsp of ground Cinnamon optional
Salt as well as Pepper to taste

INSTRUCTIONS

1. Cut the pleasant potatoes throughout meagerly. Use a mandolin or a sustenance processor.

2. Splash the pleasant potato cuts in infection water for 30 minutes.

3. Channel and motion of congratulations dry the cuts entirely. Rehash on different occasions till totally dry.

4. This as well as essential breakthrough to ensure fresh chips.

5. Toss the sweet potato cuts with olive oil, salt and pepper, and cinnamon, guaranteeing each cut is covered with oil.

6. Daintily oil the air rotisserie container.

7. In groups, air sear the sweet potatoes at 390F for 20 mins, providing the bushel a decent shake each 7 to 8 mins for food preparation.

8. On the off possibility that it still not fresh, air sear for an additional 5 minutes.

9. Offer hot with ketchup.

Banana Chips

Serving: 4
Time: Preparation Time: 15mins, Prepare Time: 25mins

INGREDIENTS

- 3-4 computers Raw Banana

- 1-- tsp Salt
- 1/2 - tsp Turmeric powder
- 1/2 - tsp Chaat masala
- 1-- tsp Oil

INSTRUCTIONS

1. Strip the bananas and maintain aside. Establish a mix of water, turmeric powder, as well as salt.
2. Cut cuts of banana in this blend. It will certainly keep the bananas to show darkish and also moreover will provide very first rate yellow shading.
3. Keep bananas absorbed this mix for five - 10 minutes. Network the water and dry the chips.
4. Apply little oil on chips to abstain from staying of banana contributes Air-fryer. Pre-heat the air fryer at one hundred eighty ranges for 5 minutes.
5. Air-fry the chips for 15 min at a hundred as well as eighty rates. Include salt and also go to masala.
6. Shop it in an impermeable box as well as serve as soon as possible.

Seasoned Chickpeas

Servings: 4
Time: Preparation Time: 10mins, Cook Time: 20mins

INGREDIENTS

- 1 15 - ounce can chickpeas
- 2 - tablespoons olive oil
- 1 - batch Homemade Cattle ranch Seasoning
- 1 - tsp sea salt
- 2 - tablespoons lemon juice

INSTRUCTIONS

1. In a little bowl, hurl together the chickpeas and 1 tbsp of the olive oil. Air-fryer at 400F for 15 minutes

2. Exchange the chickpeas back to your little dish, as well as toss in the remainder of the oil in addition to the Cattle ranch Spices, salt, and also lemon capture so the beans get good as well as covered.
3. Exchange the chickpeas back to your air fryer crate and cook at 350F for 5 extra minutes.
4. Offer now, or cool totally as well as after that store in a hermetically sealed area.

Corn Tortilla Chips

Serving: 2
Time: Prep Time: 3mins, Cook Time: 5mins

INGREDIENTS

- 8 - Corn Tortillas
- 1 - tbsp olive oil
- Salt to taste

INSTRUCTIONS

1. Preheat Philips Air-fryer to 200C.
2. Cut corn tortillas right into triangulars with a pointy blade.
3. Brush with olive oil.
4. Spot half of the tortilla sections in twine bushel and also air-fry for 3 minutes.
5. Rehash with the 2nd collection.
6. Sprinkle with salt as well as serve.
7. The top-notch component about this elements is the little level of oil made use of, as well as the capacity to regulate the step of sodium inside the chips.
8. This more advantageous adjustment of tortilla chips can be a success at your following amassing and also suitable for after college treats.

Apple Chips

Serving: 1
Time: Prep Time: 10mins, Prepare Time: 15mins

INGREDIENTS
- 1 - tool apple
- 1/4 - tsp. cinnamon
- 1/4 - tsp. nutmeg

INSTRUCTIONS
1. Preheat Air Fryer to 375 ° F.
2. Daintily cut apple utilizing a mandolin or a blade.
3. In a dish, incorporate apple cuts, cinnamon as well as nutmeg.
4. Exchange prepared apple cuts to air fryer dog crate in one layer and heat for 8 mins.

Zucchini Parmesan Chips

Serving: 2
Time: Preparation Time: 18mins, Cook Time: 34mins

Ingredients
- 2 - tool sized Zucchinis
- 1 - Egg lightly defeated
- 1/2 - mug Italian-seasoned Breadcrumbs
- 1/2 - cup grated Parmesan Cheese
- 1/2 - tsp of Smoked Paprika
- Food preparation spray or mist
- Salt and also freshly fractured pepper

Instructions
1. Cut the zucchinis as daintily as achievable with a blade or a mandolin slicer.
2. Pat completely dry with a paper towel to abandon abundance wetness.
3. Beat the egg with a small spray of water, a void of salt and pepper, in a shallow dish.
4. In any type of various other superficial bowl, join the breadcrumbs, ground cheddar and also smoked paprika.

5. Dunk a zucchini minimize in the egg, and afterwards in the cheddar breadcrumbs blend.
6. Find the nibble buried cuts a cable rack. Rehash with each one of the cuts
7. Sprinkle the nibble consisted of zucchini cuts with cooking bathe or fog.
8. Spot the cuts within the bushel of the air fryer in a solitary layer, seeing to it that they do not cover.
9. Air-fryer in globs at 350° F for 8mins.

Sriracha-Honey Wings

Serving: 2
Time: Prep Time: 20mins, Cook Time: 25mins

Ingredients
- 1 - pound hen wings
- 1/4 - mug honey
- 2 - tbsps sriracha sauce
- 1 1/2 - tbsps soy sauce
- 1 - tbsp butter
- juice of 1/2 lime
- cilantro

Instructions
1. Preheat the air fryer to 360 levels F. Add the poultry wings to the air fryer bin, and also cook for half-hour, turning the hen around at ordinary durations with tongs to make certain the wings are in a similar way caramelized.
2. While the wings are cooking, upload the sauce repairings to a little bit sauce skillet and also warmth to the aspect of boiling for rounded three mins.
3. At the point when the wings are cooked, toss them in a dish with the sauce till entirely covered, sprinkle with the covering, as well as serve right now.

Crunchy deep-fried pickles

Servings: 4
Time: Preparation Time: 15mins, Cook Time: 10mins

Ingredients

- 14 - Thickly reduced dill pickle
- 1/4 - cup all objective flour
- 1/8 - tsp baking powder
- 3 - Tablespoons dark beer
- Squeeze salt
- 2 to 3 - Tablespoons water
- 2 - Tbsps corn starch
- 6 - Tsp panko bread crumbs
- 1/2 - teaspoon paprika
- Pinch chili pepper
- Oil spray for air frying
- 1/4 to 1/2 - cup vegan cattle ranch

Instructions

1. Dry the pickle cuts on a clean kitchen towel, emphasizing to completely dry each side.
2. In a little bowl, join normally helpful flour, home heating powder, dim beer, a press of salt, as well as 2 Tbsps of water. The player should be thick yet pourable, similar to waffle player.
3. Produce 2 dinner plates. On one plate, spray corn starch. On the 2nd plate, consolidate panko bread pieces, paprika, chili pepper, and an additional area of salt.
4. Presently it's an excellent opportunity to bread the pickles. Make a sequential building system on your counter with pickles, at that point cornstarch, then ale hitter, as well as after that panko mix. In situation you're air browning, put the air fryer cage toward the coating of the consecutive construction system. In case you're fricasseeing them, placed an extra plate for battered pickles.

5. One pickle at any type of given moment put the pickle cut in corn starch on each side. Faucet to remove excess corn starch. This will certainly make it less complex for the gamer to comply with the cut. Then plunge the cut in beer player, emphasizing to similarly layer it.
6. On the occasion that air browning: Place the cut right into the air fryer. Wage most of the dill pickle cuts, guaranteeing that they are in a singular also layer visible all over fryer crate. Offer a spritz with dash oil. Air burn for 8 mins at 360 levels, stopping as soon as component of the means with to flip the majority of the cuts and give an additional spritz of oil.
7. In the event that searing in skillet: Proceed battering most of the dill pickle cuts, and also place each breaded cut on the last plate. Spread the skillet in a small layer of all-natural canola oil. Contingent upon the extent of your frying pan. Broil for 3 mins on one side, flip the majority of the pickle cuts, as well as burn for an extra 1 to 2 mins, up until they are toasty darker.
8. Present with vegetable fan ranch dressing.

Parmesan Dill Fried Pickle Chips

Serving: 4
Time: Prep Time: 15mins, Prepare Time: 20mins

Instructions

- 32 - oz. jar whole big dill pickles
- 2 - eggs
- 2/3c. panko bread crumbs
- 1/3c. grated Parmesan
- 1/4 - tsp. dried dill weed

Instructions

1. Cut the expansive pickles collar to corner into 1/four" thick cuts.
2. The area between layers of paper towels and also rub completely dry.

3. In a shallow dish, defeated the eggs till clean.

4. In a re-sealable percent, include the Panko bread portions, Parmesan and dill weed and also shake till very a lot consolidated.

5. In collections of 4-five items, soak the pickle reduces right into the egg combination, being positive to leave any kind of abundance egg as well as in a while toss inside the Panko mix.

6. Include 1/2 of the included pickle chips right into the Air-fryer and also heat for 8-10 mins on the optimum expanded temperature level.

7. Get rid of from the Air-fryer and also incorporate the relaxation of the pickle chips and also assembled for eight-10 mins. Offer fast with the lively farm for diving.

Honey Garlic Wings

Serving: 2
Time: Prep Time: 10mins, Cook Time: 35mins

Ingredients

- 16 - Pieces Chicken Wings
- 3/4 - mug Potato Starch
- 1/4 - mug Clover Honey
- 1/4 - mug Butter
- 4 - Tablespoons Fresh Garlic minced
- 1/2 - tsp Kosher Salt
- 1/8 - cup Fresh Water

DIRECTIONS

1. Wash and completely dry hen wings. Include Potato Starch to a bowl as well as layer hen wings.

2. Include included poultry wings to Air Fryer.

3. Chef at 380 tiers for 25 minutes, trembling the dog crate like clockwork.

4. At the variable whilst Timer seems, prepare dinner at 4 hundred tiers for 5-10mins.

5. All pores and also skin on all wings must be dry and gleaming.

6. Warmth a bit dealt with metallic pan on low heat. Liquefy spread and also after that include garlic. Sauté the garlic for 5 minutes.

7. Include nectar as well as salt and also stew on low for round 20mins, blending like clockwork, just so the sauce does no longer devour.

8. Include numerous decreases of water complying with 15 minutes to defend Sauce from solidifying.

9. Expel chicken wings from Air Fryer as well as pour over the sauce.

Chicken Coconut Bites

Preparation time: 10 mins
Cooking time: 13 mins
Servings: 4

Ingredients:

- 2 tsps garlic powder
- 2 eggs
- Salt and black pepper to the preference
- 3/4 mug panko bread crumbs
- 3/4 cup coconut, shredded
- Food preparation spray
- 8 chicken tenders

Directions:

1. In a bowl, mix eggs with salt, pepper as well as garlic powder as well as whisk well.

2. In one more bowl, mix coconut with panko as well as mix well.

3. Dip chicken tenders in eggs mix and after that coat in coconut one well.

4. Spray poultry bites with cooking spray, place them in your air fryer's basket as well as cook them at 350 levels F for 10 minutes.

5. Arrange them on a plate and also function as an appetizer.
Delight in!

Nutrition: calories 252, fat 4, fiber 2, carbohydrates 14, protein 24

Buffalo Cauliflower Treat

Preparation time: 10 mins
Food preparation time: 15 mins
Servings: 4

Ingredients:
- 4 cups cauliflower florets
- 1 cup panko bread crumbs
- 1/4 mug butter, thawed
- 1/4 cup buffalo sauce
- Mayonnaise for offering

Instructions:
1. In a dish, mix buffalo sauce with butter and blend well.
2. Dip cauliflower florets in this mix and also layer them in panko bread crumbs.
3. Place them in your air fryer's basket as well as chef at 350 degrees F for 15 minutes.
4 Prepare them on a platter as well as offer with mayo on the side.
Delight in!

Nutrition: calories 241, fat 4, fiber 7, carbs 8, protein 4.

Banana Snack

Preparation time: 10 minutes
Cooking time: 5 mins
Servings: 8

Ingredients:
- 16 cooking mugs crust

- 1/4 mug peanut butter
- 3/4 mug delicious chocolate chips
- 1 banana, peeled off as well as cut into 16 pieces
- 1 tablespoon grease

Directions:
1. Place delicious chocolate chips in a small pot, heat up over low warm, stir until it melts and also take off heat.
2. In a dish, mix peanut butter with coconut oil and whisk well.
3. Spoon 1 teaspoon delicious chocolate mix in a cup, add 1 banana piece and top with 1 tsp butter mix
4. Repeat with the rest of the cups, place them all right into a meal that fits your air fryer, chef at 320 levels F for 5 mins, transfer to a freezer and maintain there till you serve them as a treat.
Take pleasure in!

Nourishment: calories 70, fat 4, fiber 1, carbs 10, healthy protein 1

Potato Spread

Preparation time: 10 mins
Cooking time: 10 mins
Servings: 10

Active ingredients:
- 19 ounces canned garbanzo beans, drained pipes
- 1 mug wonderful potatoes, peeled off as well as chopped
- 1/4 mug tahini
- 2 tablespoons lemon juice
- 1 tbsp olive oil
- 5 garlic cloves, diced
- 1/2 teaspoon cumin, ground
- 2 tbsps water

Instructions:

1. Place potatoes in your air fryer's basket, cook them at 360 levels F for 15 mins, cool them down, peel off, place them in your mixer and also pulse well. basket,
2. Add sesame paste, garlic, beans, lemon juice, cumin, water as well as oil and also pulse truly well.
3. Include salt and pepper, pulse again, divide right into bowls and also offer.

Mexican Apple Snack

Prep work time: 10 mins
Cooking time: 5 minutes
Servings: 4

Ingredients:

- 3 big apples, cored, peeled off and cubed
- 2 teaspoons lemon juice
- 1/4 cup pecans, chopped
- 1/2 mug dark delicious chocolate chips
- 1/2 cup tidy sugar sauce

Instructions:

1. In a dish, mix apples with lemon juice, mix as well as move to a pan that fits your air fryer.
2. Include delicious chocolate chips, pecans, sprinkle the sugar sauce, toss, present in your air fryer and also chef at 320 levels F for 5 mins.
3 Toss delicately, split right into tiny bowls and also offer as soon as possible as a snack. Enjoy!

Nutrition: calories 200, fat 4, fiber 3, carbs 20, protein 3.

Shrimp Muffins

Prep work time: 10 mins

Food preparation time: 26 mins
Servings: 6

Ingredients:

- 1 spaghetti squash, peeled and also halved
- 2 tablespoons mayonnaise
- 1 mug mozzarella, shredded
- 8 ounces shrimp, peeled off, prepared and chopped
- 1 and 1/2 cups panko
- 1 teaspoon parsley flakes
- 1 garlic clove, minced
- Salt as well as black pepper to the preference
- Cooking spray

Directions:

1. Put squash halves in your air fryer, chef at 350 degrees F for 16 mins, leave aside to cool down as well as scuff flesh right into a bowl.
2. Add salt, pepper, parsley flakes, panko, shrimp, mayo and also mozzarella and also mix well.
3. Spray a muffin tray that fits your air fryer with cooking spray and also divide squash and also shrimp mix in each cup.
4 Introduce in the fryer and cook at 360 degrees F for 10 minutes.
5. Arrange muffins on a platter as well as function as a snack.
Delight in!

Nutrition: calories 60, fat 2, fiber 0.4, carbohydrates 4, protein 4.

Zucchini Cakes

Prep work time: 10 mins
Cooking time: 12 mins
Servings: 12

Ingredients:

- Food preparation spray

- 1/2 mug dill, cut
- 1 egg
- 1/2 mug whole wheat flour
- Salt and black pepper to the taste
- 1 yellow onion, chopped
- 2 garlic cloves, diced
- 3 zucchinis, grated

Instructions:

1. In a bowl, mix zucchinis with garlic, onion, flour, salt, pepper, egg as well as dill, mix well, form tiny patties out of this mix, spray them with food preparation spray, place them in your air fryer's basket as well as chef at 370 levels F for 6 minutes on each side.
2 Serve them as a treat today.
Enjoy!

Nutrition: calories 60, fat 1, fiber 2, carbs 6, healthy protein 2.

Cauliflower Pubs

Preparation time: 10 minutes
Cooking time: 25 mins
Servings: 12

Ingredients:

- 1 huge cauliflower head, florets divided
- 1/2 cup mozzarella, shredded
- 1/4 mug egg whites
- 1 tsp Italian seasoning
- Salt and also black pepper to the taste

Directions:

1. Put cauliflower florets in your food processor, pulse well, spread on a lined baking sheet that fits your air fryer, present in the fryer as well as cook at 360 degrees F for 10 mins.

2. Transfer cauliflower to a dish, add salt, pepper, cheese, egg whites and also Italian seasoning, stir really well, spread this right into a rectangular shape frying pan that fits your air fryer, press well, introduce in the fryer and cook at 360 levels F for 15 minutes a lot more.
3. Cut into 12 bars, organize them on a plate as well as work as a snack
Take pleasure in!

Nutrition: calories 50, fat 1, fiber 2, carbs 3, healthy protein 3

Pesto Crackers

Preparation time: 10 mins
Food preparation time: 17 mins
Servings: 6

Ingredients:

- 1/2 teaspoon baking powder
- Salt and also black pepper to the taste
- 1 and also 1/4 cups flour
- 1/4 tsp basil, dried out
- 1 garlic clove, diced
- 2 tablespoons basil pesto
- 3 tablespoons butter

Directions:

1. In a bowl, mix salt, pepper, cooking powder, flour, garlic, cayenne, basil, pesto and butter and also mix until you acquire a dough.
2. Spread this dough on a lined baking sheet that fits your air fryer, introduce in the fryer at 325 degrees F and also bake for 17 minutes.
3. Leave apart to cool, reduced crackers as well as offer them as a snack.
Enjoy!

Nutrition: calories 200, fat 20, fiber 1, carbs 4, healthy protein 7

Pumpkin Muffins

Prep work time: 10 mins
Cooking time: 15 minutes
Servings: 18

Ingredients:
- 1/4 mug butter
- 3/4 cup pumpkin puree
- 2 tbsps flaxseed meal
- 1/4 cup flour
- 1/2 mug sugar
- 1/2 tsp nutmeg, ground
- 1 teaspoon cinnamon powder
- 1/2 teaspoon baking soda
- 1 egg
- 1/2 teaspoon cooking powder

Directions:
1. In a dish, mix butter with pumpkin puree and egg as well as blend well.
2 Add flaxseed dish, flour, sugar, baking soda, baking powder, nutmeg and also cinnamon as well as stir well.
3. Spoon this right into a muffin frying pan that fits your fryer introduce in the fryer at 350 levels F and also cook for 15 mins.
4. Offer muffins chilly as a snack.
Take pleasure in!

Nutrition: calories 50, fat 3, fiber 1, carbs 2, protein 2.

Zucchini Chips

Preparation time: 10 minutes
Food preparation time: 1 hour
Servings: 6

Ingredients:
- 3 zucchinis, thinly sliced
- Salt and also black pepper to the taste
- 2 tbsps olive oil
- 2 tbsps balsamic vinegar

Directions:
1. In a bowl, mix oil with vinegar, salt and also pepper as well as whisk well.
2. Include zucchini slices, throw to coat well, present in your air fryer and cook at 200 degrees F for 1 hr.
3. Offer zucchini chips cold as a treat.
Enjoy!

Nutrition: calories 40, fat 3, fiber 7, carbs 3, protein 7

Beef Jerky Snack

Preparation time: 2 hours
Food preparation time: 1 hour and also thirty minutes
Servings: 6

Ingredients:
- 2 mugs soy sauce
- 1/2 mug Worcestershire sauce
- 2 tbsps black peppercorns
- 2 tbsps black pepper
- 2 extra pounds beef round, cut

Directions:
1. In a bowl, mix soy sauce with black peppercorns, black pepper and also Worcestershire sauce and also blend well.
2. Add beef pieces, toss to coat and also leave aside in the fridge for 6 hrs.
3. Present beef rounds in your air fryer and prepare them at 370 levels F for 1 hr and also thirty minutes.
4. Transfer to a dish and also offer cool.
Delight in!

Nutrition: calories 300, fat 12, fiber 4, carbs 3, protein 8

Honey Event Wings

Preparation time: 1 hr and also 10 minutes
Cooking time: 12 mins
Servings: 8

Ingredients:
- 16 hen wings, cut in half
- 2 tbsps soy sauce
- 2 tablespoons honey
- Salt and black pepper to the preference
- 2 tbsps lime juice

Directions:
1. In a dish, mix poultry wings with soy sauce, honey, salt, pepper as well as lime juice, toss well as well as maintain in the fridge for 1 hour.
2. Transfer poultry wings to your air fryer as well as cook them at 360 levels F for 12 minutes, flipping them midway.
3 Prepare them on a plate and also act as an appetizer.
Appreciate!

Nutrition: calories 211, fat 4, fiber 7, carbohydrates 14, protein 3.

Salmon Patties

Prep work time: 10 minutes
Cooking time: 22 minutes
Servings: 4

Ingredients:
- 3 large potatoes, steamed, drained as well as mashed
- 1 big salmon fillet, skinless, boneless
- 2 tbsps parsley, sliced
- 2 tbsp dill, cut
- Salt and also black pepper to the preference
- 1 egg
- 2 tbsps bread crumbs
- Cooking spray

Directions:
1. Location salmon in your air fryer's basket and chef for 10 mins at 360 degrees F.
2. Transfer salmon to a reducing board, cool it down, flake it as well as put it in a dish.
3. Include mashed potatoes, salt, pepper, dill, parsley, egg as well as bread crumbs, stir well and shape 8 patties out of this mix.
4. Place salmon patties in your air fryer's basket, spry them with cooking oil, chef at 360 levels F for 12 mins, flipping them midway, transfer them to a plate as well as act as an appetiser.

Enjoy!

Spring Rolls

Prep work time: 10 mins
Cooking time: 25 mins
Servings: 8

Ingredients:
- 2 cups environment-friendly cabbage, shredded
- 2 yellow onions, chopped
- 1 carrot, grated
- 1/2 chili pepper, minced
- 1 tablespoon ginger, grated
- 3 garlic cloves, minced
- 1 teaspoon sugar
- Salt and also black pepper to the preference
- 1 teaspoon soy sauce
- 2 tbsps olive oil
- 10 spring roll sheets
- 2 tablespoons corn flour

- 2 tablespoons water

Instructions:
1. Heat up a pan with the oil over medium warmth, include cabbage, onions, carrots, chili pepper, ginger, garlic, sugar, salt, pepper and also soy sauce, stir well, chef for 2-3 mins, take off heat and also cool off.
2. Cut springtime roll sheets in squares, divide cabbage mix on each and roll them.
3. In a dish, mix corn flour with water, mix well as well as secure spring rolls with this mix.
4 Location spring rolls in your air fryer's basket as well as prepare them at 360 degrees F for 10 minutes.
5. Flip roll and cook them for 10 minutes much more.
6. Organize on a platter and serve them as an appetizer.
Delight in!

Nutrition: calories 214, fat 4, fiber 4, carbohydrates 12, protein 4.

Crispy Radish Chips

Prep work time: 10 mins
Cooking time: 10 mins
Servings: 4

Ingredients:
- Cooking spray
- 15 radishes, cut
- Salt and black pepper to the taste
- 1 tablespoon chives, sliced

Instructions:

1 Arrange radish pieces in your air fryer's basket, spray them with cooking oil, period with salt and also black pepper to the preference, prepare them at 350 degrees F for 10 minutes, turning them midway, transfer to bowls as well as offer with chives sprinkled ahead.
Take pleasure in!

Nutrition: calories 80, fat 1, fiber 1, carbohydrates 1, healthy protein 1.

Crab Sticks

Prep work time: 10 minutes
Food preparation time: 12 mins
Servings: 4

Ingredients:
- 10 crabsticks, cut in half
- 2 teaspoons sesame oil
- 2 tsps Cajun flavoring

Instructions:
1. Place crab sticks in a dish, add sesame oil and Cajun spices, toss, transfer them to your air fryer's basket as well as cook at 350 degrees F for 12 minutes.
Arrange on a platter as well as work as an appetizer.
Delight in!

Nourishment: calories 110, fat 0, fiber 1, carbs 4, healthy protein 2

Air Fried Dill Pickles

Prep work time: 10 minutes
Cooking time: 5 minutes
Servings: 4

Ingredients:

- 16 ounces shook dill pickles, reduced right into wedges and rub dried out
- 1/2 mug white flour
- 1 egg
- 1/4 mug milk
- 1/2 tsp garlic powder
- 1/2 teaspoon wonderful paprika
- Food preparation spray
- 1/4 cup ranch sauce

Instructions:

1. In a bowl, incorporate milk with egg as well as blend well
2. In a 2nd bowl, mix flour with salt, garlic powder as well as paprika as well as stir also.
3. Dip pickles in flour, then in egg mix and also once again in flour as well as position them in your air fryer.
4 Oil them with cooking spray, cook pickle wedges at 400 levels F for 5 mins, transfer to a dish as well as offer with cattle ranch sauce on the side.
Appreciate!

Nutrition: calories 109, fat 2, fiber 2, carbs 10, protein 4.

Chickpeas Snack

Prep work time: 10 mins
Food preparation time: 10 mins
Servings: 4

Ingredients:
- 15 ounces tinned chickpeas, drained pipes
- 1/2 tsp cumin, ground
- 1 tablespoon olive oil
- 1 tsp smoked paprika
- Salt and also black pepper to the taste

Directions:

1. In a dish, mix chickpeas with oil, cumin, paprika, salt as well as pepper, throw to coat, put them in your fryer's basket and cook at 390 degrees F for 10 mins.
2. Divide into bowls and act as a treat. Delight in!

Nourishment: calories 140, fat 1, fiber 6, carbs 20, protein 6

Sausage Balls

Prep work time: 10 mins
Food preparation time: 15 minutes
Servings: 9

Ingredients:
- 4 ounces sausage meat, ground
- Salt and black pepper to the taste
- 1 teaspoon sage
- 1/2 tsp garlic, minced
- 1 tiny onion, cut
- 3 tbsps breadcrumbs

Directions:

1. In a dish, mix sausage with salt, pepper, sage, garlic, onion and breadcrumbs, mix well and shape tiny balls out of this mix.
2. Put them in your air fryer's basket, cook at 360 levels F for 15 mins, split right into bowls and function as a treat.
Enjoy!

Nutrition: calories 130, fat 7, fiber 1, carbs 13, healthy protein 4

Tangy Chicken Dip

Prep work time: 10 mins
Cooking time: 25 mins
Servings: 10

Ingredients:
- 3 tablespoons butter, thawed
- 1 mug yogurt
- 12 ounces cream cheese
- 2 mugs poultry meat, prepared and also shredded
- 2 tsps curry powder
- 4 scallions, chopped
- 6 ounces Monterey jack cheese, grated
- 1/3 cup raisins
- 1/4 cup cilantro, sliced
- 1/2 cup almonds, sliced
- Salt and black pepper to the taste
- 1/2 mug chutney

Directions:
1. In a dish mix lotion cheese with yogurt and whisk using your mixer.
2. Include curry powder, scallions, hen meat, raisins, cheese, cilantro, salt and pepper and mix every little thing.
3. Spread this into a baking dish that hand your air fryer, sprinkle almonds on the top, area in your air fryer, cook at 300 levels for 25 mins, split right into bowls, top with chutney as well as work as an appetizer. Take pleasure in!

Nutrition: calories 240, fat 10, fiber 2, carbs 24, protein 12

Popcorn Snack

Prep work time: 5 mins
Food preparation time: 10 minutes
Servings: 4

Ingredients:
- 2 tbsps corn kernels
- 2 and 1/2 tbsps butter
- 2 ounces brownish sugar

Directions:

1 Put corn kernels in your air fryer's pan, chef at 400 levels F for 6 minutes, move them to a tray, spread and also leave apart for now.
2. Heat up a pan over low heat, include butter, thaw it, sugarcoat and also stir until it dissolves.
3. Add popcorn, toss to layer, take off warm as well as spread on the tray once more.
4. Cool, divide into bowls and act as a snack. Appreciate!

Nutrition: calories 70, fat 0.2, fiber 0, carbohydrates 1, healthy protein 1.

Roasted Bell Pepper Rolls

Prep work time: 10 mins
Food preparation time: 10 mins
Servings: 8

Directions:
- 1 yellow bell pepper, cut in half
- 1 orange bell pepper, cut in half
- Salt as well as black pepper to the preference
- 4 ounces feta cheese, fallen apart
- 1 eco-friendly onion, cut
- 2 tbsps oregano, cut

Instructions:
1. In a dish, mix cheese with onion, oregano, salt as well as pepper as well as blend well.
2. Area bell pepper fifty percents in your air fryer's basket, chef at 400 levels F for 10 mins, transfer to a reducing board, cool as well as peel off.
3. Split cheese mix on each bell pepper fifty percent, roll, safe with toothpicks, organize on a plate as well as act as an appetiser. Appreciate!

Nourishment: calories 170, fat 1, fiber 2, carbohydrates 8, healthy protein 5

Dinner

Rib Eye Steak

Servings: 4
Time: Preparation Time: 15mins, Prepare Time: 20mins

INGREDIENTS

- 1 - tbsp steak rub
- 1 - tbsp olive oil

INSTRUCTIONS

1. Press the Power Switch as well as exchange food preparation time to 4 mins at 4 hundred phases to pre-heat.
2. Period the steak on the 2 elements with rub as well as olive oil.
3. Area steak within the Fry Basket.
4. Press the M Switch. Want to the Steak Symbol.
5. Press the Power Switch and also profession food preparation time to 6.14 mins at 400 phases.
7. Complying with 7 mins, turn the steak.
8. At the factor whilst clock is executed, remove steak from the Power Air Fryer XL.
9. Allow leisure for 10 mins prior to reducing and also offering.
Nourishment Details: Calories 418g, Fat 10g, Carbs 84g, Sugars 50g, Healthy Protein 3g

Hen Parmesan

Servings: 4
Time: Preparation Time: 20mins, Prepare Time: 30mins

INGREDIENTS

- 8 - oz poultry bust
- 6 - tablespoon skilled breadcrumbs
- 2 - tablespoon grated Parmesan cheese
- 1 - tablespoon butter
- 6 - tablespoon lowered fat mozzarella cheese
- 1/2 - mug marinara
- cooking spray

INSTRUCTIONS

1. Dash the lolled gently with bathe.
2. Settle breadcrumbs and also parmesan cheddar in a dish.
3. Liquify the margarine in any type of various other dish.
4. Daintily clean the unravel onto the chicken, then dive right into breadcrumb combination.
5. At the variable whilst the air fryer is prepared, area 2 parts inside the container and also wash the leading with oil.
6. Prepare 6 mins, turn as well as leading each with 1 tablespoon sauce as well as 1/2 tablespoon of ruined mozzarella cheddar.
7. Prepare 3 additional mins or till cheddar is softened.
8. Deposit as well as protect warmth, rehash with the leisure of the 2 items.

Turkey & Cheese Calzone

Servings: 4.
Time: Preparation Time: 10mins, Prepare Time: 10mins.

INGREDIENTS

- Homemade Pizza Dough or Store Bought
- 4 - Tablespoon Homemade Tomato Sauce.
- Extra Turkey brownish meat shredded.
- 100g - Cheddar Cheese.
- 25g - Mozzarella Cheese grated.
- 25g - Back Bacon diced.

- 1 - Big Egg defeated.
- 1 - Tablespoon Tomato Puree.
- 1 - Tsp Oregano.
- 1 - Tsp Basil.
- 1 - Tsp Thyme.
- Salt & Pepper.

INSTRUCTIONS

1. Pre-heat your Air Fryer to 180c.
2. Begin by exposing your pizza blend with the objective that they are the procedure of little pizzas. In a little incorporating dish consist of each of the flavorings equally as the tomato sauce and also puree.
3. Using a food preparation brush consist of a layer of tomato sauce to your pizza bases guaranteeing that it does not truly get in touch with the side with a 1cm room.
4. Layer up your pizza with your turkey, bacon and also cheddar to the opposite.
5. With the 1cm opening around your pizza base as well as using your food preparation brush once again, brush with ruined egg. Wrinkle your pizza base over so it resembles a raw Cornish pale and also all area that is currently evident of the pizza combination to be cleaned with even more egg.
6. Area airborne Fryer for 10 mins at 180c.
7. Offer.

Turkey with Maple Mustard

Luster

Servings: 6.
Time: Preparation Time: 25mins, Prepare Time: 45mins.

INGREDIENTS
- 2 - tsps olive oil.
- 5 - extra pound entire turkey bust.
- 1 - tsp dried out thyme.
- 1/2 - tsp dried out sage.
- 1/2 - tsp smoked paprika.
- 1 - tsp salt.

- 1/2 - tsp fresh ground black pepper.
- 1/4 - mug syrup.
- 2 - tbsp Dijon mustard.
- 1 - tbsp butter.

INSTRUCTIONS

1. Pre warm air fryer to 350°F.
2. Brush the olive oil all over throughout the turkey breast.
3. Settle the thyme, sage, paprika, salt as well as pepper and also massage the beyond the turkey breast with the taste mix.
4. Exchange the ready turkey breast to the air fryer pet crate as well as air-broil at 350°F for 25 mins.
5. Transform the turkey breast on its side as well as air-sear for an extra 12 mins.
6. Transform the turkey breast on the other hand side as well as air-broil for an added 12 mins.
7. The within temperature level of the turkey breast need to attain 165°F when entirely prepared.
8. While the turkey is air-singing, combine the syrup, mustard and also margarine in a little frying pan.
9. At the factor when the devising time is, return the turkey breast to an honest placement as well as clean the finish all over throughout the turkey.
10. Air-sear for a last 5 mins, till the skin is happily sautéed and also fresh.
11. Offer the turkey an opportunity to remainder, inexactly climbed with aluminum foil, for someplace around 5 mins prior to reducing as well as offering.

Pork Taquitos

Servings: 10.
Time: Preparation Time: 25mins, Prepare Time: 35mins.

INGREDIENTS

- 3 - mugs prepared shredded pork tenderloin.
- 2 1/2 - mugs fat cost-free shredded mozzarella.
- 10 - little flour tortillas.
- 1 - lime.
- Food preparation spray.

INSTRUCTIONS

1. Preheat air fryer to 380 phases.
2. Sprinkle lime capture over red meat and also tenderly mix about.
3. Microwave 5 tortillas at any type of offered 2nd with a soaked paper towel over it for 10 secs, to relax.
4. Consist of 3 oz. Of beef as well as 1/four level of cheddar to a tortilla.
5. Strongly and also tenderly move up the tortillas.
6. Line tortillas on a lubed aluminum foil covered box.
7. Dash a reasonable layer of cooking bathe over tortillas.
8. Air Fry for 7-10 mins till tortillas are a very excellent shading, turning a component of the way using.
9. 2 taquitos according to offering WW SP - 8.
10. Be that as it has the ability to, at the off threat which you do not have an air fryer, they can similarly be warmed within the variety for 7 - 10 mins on 375 phases.

Pork Chops

Servings: 4
Time: Preparation Time: 30mins, Prepare Time: 54mins

INGREDIENTS

- 1/2 - mug Dijon mustard
- 4 - pork loin chops
- 1 - mug Italian bread crumbs
- 1/2 - tsp salt
- 1/2 - tsp black pepper
- 1/4 - tsp chili pepper

DIRECTIONS

1. Pre-heat the griddle to prepare.
2. Spread out the mustard evenly on both sides of the pork cleaves.
3. In a superficial meal, sign up with the bread scraps, salt, dark pepper, and also cayenne. Dig the pork slashes in the items so both sides are equitably covered.
4. Identify the pork cleaves on a cake rack established over a home heating sheet. Find the sheet in the griddle around 4 creeps from the warming element.
5. Chef, transforming when, till the pork cleaves are great dark tinted. Remove from the griddle as well as offer immediately.

Crispy Breaded Pork Chops

Servings: 6
Time: Preparation Time: 15mins, Prepare Time: 15mins

INGREDIENTS

- olive oil spray
- 3/4 - inch thick facility
- kosher salt
- 1 - huge egg
- 1/2 - mug panko crumbs
- 1/3 - mug smashed cornflakes crumbs
- 2 - tablespoon grated parmesan cheese
- 1 1/4 - tsp wonderful paprika
- 1/2 - tsp garlic powder
- 1/2 - tsp onion powder
- 1/4 - tsp chili powder
- 1/8 - tsp black pepper

INSTRUCTIONS

1. Period red meat cuts on the 2 elements with fifty percent of tsp fit salt.
2. Identify the subdued egg in a few other.

3. Dive the meat right into the egg, already item mix.

4. Precisely when the air fryer is prepared, region 3 of the cuts right into the ready area and also spray the leading with oil.

5. Prepare 12mins transforming midway, spraying both attributes with oil. Put apart as well as repeat with the last.

Chinese Salt & Pepper Pork Chops

Servings: 2
Time: Preparation Time: 10mins, Prepare Time: 15mins

INGREDIENTS

- Pork Chops
- 1 - Egg White
- 1/2 - tsp Sea Salt
- 1/4 - tsp Fresh Ground Black Pepper
- 3/4 - mug Potato Starch
- 1 - Oil Mister
- Str Fry
- 2 - Jalapeño Pepper stems gotten rid of
- 2 - Scallions
- 2 - Tablespoons Canola Oil
- 1 - tsp Sea Salt
- 1/4 - tsp Newly Ground Black Pepper
- Cast Iron Poultry Fryer

DIRECTIONS

1. Layer Air Fryer Basket with a lightweight layer of Oil.

2. In a tool dish, blend jointly egg white, salt as well as pepper till foamy.

3. Cut beef slashes right into cutlet parts, leaving a little on the bones and also rub completely dry. Include red meat reduce sections to egg white mix.

4. Season for no much less than 20 mins.

5. Exchange pork slashes an extensive dish as well as incorporate Potato Starch.

6. Dig the pork slashes thru the Potato Starch entirely.

7. Get rid of beef as well as notification right into arranged Air Fryer Basket. Naturally shower red meat with Oil.

8. Prepare at 360 phases for 9mins, trembling the bushel on a regular basis as well as bathing with oil in between drinks.

9. Prepare an additional 6 mins at 400 phases, or till the pork is dark tinted and also company.

Stromboli

Servings: 4
Time: Preparation Time: 10mins, Prepare Time: 20mins

INGREDIENTS

- 3 -mug cheddar cheese
- 0.75 - mug Mozzarella cheese
- 0.3 - extra pound prepared pork
- 3 - ounce red bell peppers
- 1 - egg yolk
- 1 - tbsp milk

DIRECTIONS

1. Roll the batter out till 1/4 inch thick.

2. Layer the pork, cheddar as well as peppers on one side of the batter. Fold over to secure.

3. Integrate the egg and also milk as well as comb the batter.

4. Identify the stromboli right into the Fry Basket and also find it right into the Power Air Fryer XL.

5. Press the M Switch. Seek to the Hen Symbol.

6. Press the Power Switch and also customize cooking time to 15 mins at 360 levels.

7. At routine periods, carefully ip stromboli over.

Beef Empanadas

Servings: 8
Time: Preparation Time: 10mins, Prepare Time: 20mins

INGREDIENTS

- 8 - Goya empanada discs
- 1 - mug picadillo
- 1 - egg white
- 1 - tsp water

INSTRUCTIONS

1. Sprinkle the pet crate freely with food preparation shower.
2. Place 2 tablespoon of picadillo inside the focal element of every plate.
3. Fold right into the same components and also make use of a fork to secure the edges.
4. Rehash with the leisure of the batter.
5. Blend the egg whites with water, at that element brush the highest possible elements of the empanadas.
6. Prepare 2 or 3 at any type of provided minute big all rounded fryer 8 mins, or till excellent.
7. Remove from cozy temperature level and also rehash with the last empanadas.

Cheese Burgers

Servings: 4
Time: Preparation Time: 10mins, Prepare Time: 10mins

INGREDIENTS

- 1 - Tbsp Worcestershire sauce
- 1 - tsp Maggi spices sauce
- fluid smoke
- 1/2 - tsp garlic powder
- 1/2 - tsp onion powder
- 1/2 - tsp salt
- 1/2 - tsp ground black pepper
- 1 - tsp parsley
- 500g - hamburger
- 5 pieces of American Cheese

INSTRUCTIONS

1. Sprinkle the cage freely with food preparation shower.
2. Place 2 tablespoon of picadillo inside the focal aspect of every plate.
3. Fold right into similar components as well as use a fork to secure the edges.
4. Rehash with the leisure of the batter.
5. Blend the egg whites with water, at that element brush the highest possible elements of the empanadas.
6. Prepare 2 or 3 at any kind of provided minute large all rounded fryer 8 mins, or till excellent.
7. Eliminate from cozy temperature level as well as rehash with the last empanadas.

Roasted Stuffed Peppers

Servings: 4
Time: Prep Time: 15mins, Prepare Time: 25mins

INGREDIENTS

- 2 - tool green peppers
- 1/2 - medium onion
- 1 - clove garlic
- 1 - teaspoon olive oil
- 8 - ounces lean ground beef
- 1/2 - mug tomato sauce
- 1 - tsp Worcestershire sauce
- 1/2 - teaspoon salt
- 1/2 - teaspoon black pepper
- 4 - ounces cheddar cheese

INSTRUCTIONS

1. Warmth air fryer consistent with headings
2. Sauté the onion and also garlic within the olive oil in a little nonstick frying pan till fantastic and eliminate from burner to chill.

3. Mix the hamburger, cooked vegetables, 1/4 box tomato sauces, Worcestershire, salt as well as pepper as well as a massive portion of the destroyed cheddar in a tool dish.

4. Dividers and things the pepper elements - peak with superior tomato sauce and also cheddar.

5. Coordinate significant all round fryer cage and also air-fryer or prepare till meat is cooked via - 15 to 20mins.

Meatloaf

Servings: 3

Time: Prep Time: 10mins, Prepare Time: 22mins

INGREDIENTS

- 1 - pound lean hamburger
- 1/2 - medium onion
- 1/3c - Kellog's corn flakes cumbs
- 1-2 - tsp salt
- 1-2 - tsp fresh ground black pepper
- 1 - tsp minced garlic
- 8 -oz tomato sauce
- 1 - tsp dried out basil
- 5 - Tbsp Heinz reduced-sugar ketchup
- 3 - tsp Splenda brownish sugar mix
- 1 - Tablespoon Worcestershire sauce
- 1/2 - Tablespoon gently dried Parsley

INSTRUCTIONS

1. Lower onion to desired dimension

2. Join flooring meat, onion, corn portions scraps, salt, pepper, garlic and around 6oz of the tomato sauce. Blend correctly.

3. Take you are smaller sized than expected component recipe if making use of a frying pan and utilize a paper towel to daintily layer within with oil.

4. Split your meat combination into 2, at that point area into the part box.

5. Make your layer by using ending up being a participant of the 2oz of tomato sauce.

6. Faded sugar ketchup, darkish-colored sugar blend, as well as Worcestershire sauce.

7. Brush the finish on the top as well as on the sides of your meatloaves.

8. Area amounts into your preheated air fryer.

9. Air sear at 360 rates for 20mins, protecting against 2 times thru cooking to re-coat the amounts

10. Remove amounts from air fryer as well as quick spray the hacked parsley on the top.

Country Fried Steak

Serving: 1

Time: Prep Time: 10mins, Prepare Time: 15mins

INGREDIENTS

- 3 -eggs, defeated
- 1 - mug flour
- 1 - cup Panko
- 1 - teaspoon onion powder
- 1 - tsp Garlic powder
- 1 - tsp salt
- 1 - tsp pepper
- 6 - ounce ground sausage meat
- 2 - tbsp flour
- 2 - cup milk
- 1 - tsp pepper

INSTRUCTIONS

1. Period the panko with the flavors

2. Dig the steak in a certain order. Flour, egg, and also ready panko

3. Spot the breaded steak right into the dog crate of the Power Air-fryer and also close.

4. Press the M to catch the Default temperature of 370 F and also set the ideal opportunity for 12 mins. Press the power catch

5. When the clock has slipped by leaving the steak as well as present with pound potatoes and also wiener sauce.

6. In a container prepare the wiener until well done. Network fat; hold 2 tbsp in the recipe.

7. Include the flour to the container with a frankfurter, mix until all the flour is integrated

8. Progressively assimilate the milk. Mix over a prescription heat till the milk enlarges

9. Period with pepper. Cook for 3 mins to cook out the flour.

Fajita Chicken

Servings: 4
Time: Preparation Time: 15mins, Prepare Time: 15mins

INGREDIENTS

- 4 - poultry busts
- 2 - tablespoon olive oil
- 2 - tablespoon FAJITA flavoring
- 1/2 - each red yellow as well as orange pepper
- 1 - red onion cut
- 1/2 - mug shredded cheese
- Cilantro
- Salsa as well as sour lotion

INSTRUCTIONS

1. Preheat Air fryer if essential to the pre-set poultry selection or 380 levels.

2. Make cuts over every hen breast.

3. Scrub your poultry breasts with olive oil as well as fajita flavor and also later readied to the side.

4. Area cuts of chile peppers as well as red onions inside each cut.

5. Detect the poultry recognizable all over fryer veggie side searching for.

6. Prepare hen for 15 minutes.

7. Remove from the air fryer and also area on a product sheet protected preparing frying pan.

8. Leading each little hen with a lot of cheddar.

9. Establish your cooktop to scorch above. Prepare poultry till the cheddar is softened.

10. Eliminate from cooktop and also existing with some cilantro, salsa, as well as sharp lotion.

Mediterranean Veggies

Servings: 4
Time: Preparation Time: 5mins, Prepare Time: 20mins

INGREDIENTS

- 50g - Cherry Tomatoes
- 1 - Big Courgette
- 1 - Environment-friendly Pepper
- 1 - Big Parsnip
- 1 - Tool Carrot
- 1 - Tsp Mixed Herbs
- 2 - Tablespoon Honey
- 1 - Tsp Mustard
- 2 - Tsp Garlic Puree
- 6 - Tablespoon Olive Oil
- Salt & Pepper

INSTRUCTIONS

1. In the base of your Air-fryer reduced up the courgette as well as environment-friendly pepper.

2. Strip as well as shakers the parsnip as well as carrot as well as consist of the cherry tomatoes whole while still on the creeping plant for added taste.

3. Sprinkle with 3 tbsps of olive oil and also chef for 15 mins at 180c,

4. At the same time, stimulate the rest of your mendings right into an Air-fryer secure home heating meal.

5. At the factor when the veggies are done exchange them from the base of the Air-fryer right into the home heating recipe as well as drink well with the objective that each of the veggies is shrouded in the marinate.

6. Sprinkle with rather even more salt as well as pepper as well as chef for 5 mins on 200c.

7. Offer.

Fried Tomatoes with Sriracha Mayo

Servings: 4
Time: Preparation Time: 15mins, Prepare Time: 15mins

INGREDIENTS

- 3 - environment-friendly tomatoes
- salt as well as newly ground black pepper
- 1/3 - mug flour
- 2 - eggs
- 1/2 - mug buttermilk
- 1 - mug panko breadcrumbs
- 1 - mug cornmeal
- fresh thyme sprigs or sliced fresh chives
- Sriracha Mayo:
- 1/2 - mug mayo
- 1 to 2 - tbsps sriracha warm sauce
- 1 - tbsp milk

INSTRUCTIONS

1. Cut the tomatoes in 1/4- inch cuts. Rub them completely dry with a pristine kitchen area towel and also period freely with salt as well as pepper.

2. Establish an excavating terminal using 3 superficial recipes.

3. Detect the flour generally superficial meal, combine the eggs as well as buttermilk in the 2nd recipe, as well as sign up with the flour as well as cornmeal in the 3rd meal.

4. Pre-heat the air fryer to 400ºF.

5. Dig the tomato cuts in flour to layer on both sides.

6. Then soak them right into the egg mix finally push them right into the breadcrumbs to layer all sides of the tomato.

7. Dash or comb the air-fryer container with olive oil.

8. Exchange 3 to 4 tomato cuts right into the container as well as shower the top with olive oil.

9. Air-sear the tomatoes at 400ºF for 8 mins.

10. While the tomatoes are cooking, make the sriracha mayo. Settle the mayo, 1 tbsp of the Sriracha warm sauce as well as milk in a little dish.

11. At the factor when the tomatoes are done, exchange them to an air conditioning shelf or a plate taken care of with paper towels so the base does not obtain mushy.

12. Offer the fricasseed environment-friendly tomatoes warm with the sriracha mayo as a second thought.

13. Period one last time with salt as well as crisply ground dark pepper as well as cutting with sprigs of brand-new thyme or reduced brand-new chives.

Ranch Fish Fillets

Servings: 4
Time: Preparation Time: 5mins, Prepare Time: 15mins

INGREDIENTS

- 3/4 - mug bread crumbs or Panko or smashed cornflakes
- 1 30g - package completely dry ranch-style clothing mix
- 2 1/2 - tbsps grease
- 2 - eggs defeated
- 4 - tilapia salmon or various other fish fillets
- lemon wedges to garnish

DIRECTIONS

1. Pre-heat your air fryer to 180 phases C.
2. Mix the panko/breadcrumbs as well as the ranch clothing integrate.
3. Consist of the oil and also maintain mixing till the mix appears to be unfastened as well as fragile.
4. Dive the fish filets right into the egg, providing the wealth flow a danger to off.
5. Dunk the fish filets right into the nibble blend, looking for to layer them just as well as all with each other.
6. Place right into your air fryer carefully.
7. Prepare for 12-13 mins, section upon the density of the filets.
8. Remove and also offer. Squash the lemon wedges over the fish whenever wanted.

Turkey & Cheese Calzone

Servings: 4
Time: Preparation Time: 10mins, Prepare Time: 10mins

INGREDIENTS

- 4 - Tablespoon Homemade Tomato Sauce
- Extra Turkey brownish meat shredded
- 100g - Cheddar Cheese
- 25g - Mozzarella Cheese grated
- 25g - Back Bacon diced
- 1 - Big Egg defeated
- 1 - Tablespoon Tomato Puree
- 1 - Tsp Oregano
- 1 - Tsp Basil
- 1 - Tsp Thyme
- Salt & Pepper

DIRECTIONS

1. Pre-heat your Air Fryer to 180c.
2. Begin by exposing your pizza batter with the objective that they are the period of little pizzas.

3. In a little incorporating dish consist of each of the spices equally as the tomato sauce as well as puree.
4. Using a food preparation brush consist of a layer of tomato sauce to your pizza bases guaranteeing that it does not actually speak to the side with a 1cm area.
5. Layer up your pizza with your turkey, bacon, as well as cheddar to the opposite side.
6. With the 1cm opening around your pizza base and also using your food preparation brush one more time, brush with ruined egg.
7. Overlap your pizza base over so it resembles a raw Cornish pale and also all-region that is presently distinct of the pizza mix to be cleaned with even more egg.
8. A place airborne Fryer for 10 mins at 180c.
9. Offer.

Fish n Chips Sandwich

Servings: 4
Time: Preparation Time: 5mins, Prepare Time: 15mins

INGREDIENTS

- 4 - little cod fillets
- salt as well as pepper
- 2 - tablespoon flour
- 40g - dried out breadcrumbs
- spray oil
- 250g - icy peas
- 1 - tablespoon creme fraiche
- 10-- 12 - capers
- press of lemon juice
- 4 - bread rolls

INSTRUCTIONS

1. Pre-heat the Optimum HealthyFry Air Fryer.
2. Take every one of the cod filets, period with salt and also pepper as well as delicately dirt within the flour.

3. Then roll quickly in the breadcrumbs. The concept is to obtain a moderate superimposing of breadcrumbs on the fish as opposed to a thick layer.

4. Consist of a number of showers of oil sprinkle to the base of the fryer bushel.

5. Find the cod filets ahead as well as chef supper at the fish placement (200c) for 15mins.

6. While the fish is cooking, chef supper the peas in gurgling water for 2 or 3 mins on the hob or within the microwave.

7. Network as well as afterwards contribute to a blender or food processor with the creme fraiche, techniques as well as lemon juice to preference. Battery till combined.

8. When the fish has actually prepared, eliminate it from the HealthyFry Air Fryer and also begin layering your sandwich with the bread, fish as well as pea puree.

Potato Bake Style

Servings: 3
Time: Preparation Time: 10mins, Prepare Time: 35mins

INGREDIENTS

- 3 - pleasant potatoes
- 1 - tbsp olive oil
- 1-2 - tsps kosher salt

DIRECTIONS

1. Wash your wonderful potatoes and also afterwards make air spaces with a fork inside the potatoes.

2. Spray them with the olive oil and also salt, at that variable rub consistently at the potatoes.

3. When the potatoes are buried area them right into the cage for the Air Fryer and also see right into the gadget.

4. Leading along with your leading options

Spicy Fish Road Tacos with Sriracha Slaw

Servings: 3
Time: Preparation Time: 35mins, Prepare Time: 55mins

INGREDIENTS

- Sriracha Slaw:
- 1/2 - mug mayo
- 2 - tbsps rice vinegar
- 1 - tsp sugar
- 2 - ts sriracha chili sauce
- 5 - mugs environment-friendly cabbage
- 1/4 - mug shredded carrots
- 2 - scallions, sliced
- salt as well as ground black pepper

Tacos:

- 1/2 - mug flour
- 1 - tsp chili powder
- 1/2 - tsp ground cumin
- 1 - tsp salt
- fresh ground black pepper
- 1/2 - tsp cooking powder
- 1 - egg, defeated
- 1/4 - mug milk
- 1 - mug breadcrumbs
- 12 - ounces snapper fillets
- 1 - tsp canola or grease
- 6 - flour tortillas
- 1 - lime, reduced right into wedges

INSTRUCTIONS

1. Begin by making the sriracha slaw. Sign up with the mayo, rice vinegar, sugar, and also sriracha sauce in a large dish. Mix well and also consist of the eco-friendly cabbage, carrots, as well as scallions.

2. Settle the flour, bean stew powder, cumin, salt, pepper and also preparing powder in a dish. Consist of the egg and also milk as well as mix till the gamer is smooth. Find the breadcrumbs in superficial recipe.

3. Cut the fish filets right into 1-inch vast sticks, around 4-inches in size. You should certainly have about 12 fish sticks outright. Dive the fish penetrates the player, covering all sides.

4.Pre-heat the air fryer to 400°F.

5. Bath the protected fish remains with oil on all sides. Shower or brush within the air fryer container with oil and also exchange the fish to the bushel. Detect the very same variety of sticks as you can in one layer, leaving a little space around each stick. Find any kind of exceptional sticks on the top, contrary to the major layer.

6. While the fish is air-browning, cozy the tortilla coverings either in a 350°F griddle confined by aluminum foil or in a frying pan with a little oil over medium-high heat for numerous mins. Overlay the tortillas fifty-fifty and also maintain them cozy up until the remainder of the tortillas and also fish are prepared.

7. To gather the tacos, area 2 little bits of the fish in every tortilla covering and also top with the sriracha slaw. Press the lime wedge over leading as well as dive in.

Vegetarian Southwestern Egg Rolls with Avocado Ranch

Servings: 8
Time: Preparation Time: 20mins, Prepare Time: 15mins

INGREDIENTS

- 1/4 - red onion
- 2-3 - garlic cloves
- 16 - egg roll wrappers
- 1/2 - red pepper
- 1/2 - yellow pepper
- 1/2 - orange pepper
- 1/4 - mug shredded cheese
- 8 - oz low-sodium black beans
- 1 - can diced tomatoes and also chilis
- 1 - mug icy bit corn
- 2 - tsps cilantro cut
- 1/2 - lime juice of
- 1/4 - package Taco Spices
- cooking oil
- mug of water
- Avocado Ranch Dip
- 8 - oz sour lotion I made use of fat-free
- 1 - avocado

INSTRUCTIONS

1. Heat a frying pan on medium-high heat. Consist of the garlic and also onions. Prepare for 2-3 mins up until great smelling.

2. Include most of the peppers to the frying pan. Mix well. Prepare for 1-2 mins

3. Consist of the dark beans, corn, tomatoes, as well as cheddar. Prepare for 2-3 mins.

4. Bath the brand-new lime capture throughout. Consist of the cilantro as well as taco flavor. Mix.

5. Lay the egg step wrappers on a degree surface area. Dunk a food preparation brush in water. Layer each of the egg step wrappers with the damp brush along the sides. This will certainly decrease the outdoors layer and also make it less complex to roll.

6. Use 2 egg actions for each. I increased roll the egg relocates to maintain them from spilling. On the occasion that the brand name of egg relocation wrappers you got is totally thick, you might simply require one wrapper as well as no engaging factor to flex over.

7. Strain the mix right into each of the wrappers.

8. Wrinkle the wrappers slantingly to shut. Press well on the region with the dental filling, container it to validate it establish. Overlay in the left and also ideal sides as triangulars. Overlay the last layer over the leading to shut. Make use of the food preparation brush to damp the area and also safeguard it establish.

9. Strain the egg folds up right into the container of the Air Fryer.

10. Prepare for 8 mins at 380 levels. Turn the egg rolls. Prepare for an added 4 mins. Amazing prior to offering.

Crunchy Onion Rings

Servings: 1
Time: Preparation Time: 5mins, Prepare Time: 10mins

INGREDIENTS

- 1 - Mug Gluten Free Oats
- 1 - Tool Onion
- 1 - Big Egg defeated
- Salt & Pepper

INSTRUCTIONS

1. Pre-heat your air fryer to 180c.

2. Detect your ruined egg in a little dish.

3. Using a food cpu or mixer battery your oats right into great breadcrumbs so they look like a thick flour. Find them right into a dish.

4. Cut your onion right into whole cuts as you imagine within an onion ring to be.

5. Press out the rings onto your hacking board and also afterwards dunk in the oats, then in the egg and also afterwards one more time right into the oats.

6. Place obvious all over fryer for 8 mins on 180c.

7. Offer.

Crab Sticks

Servings: 24
Time: Preparation Time: 10mins, Prepare Time: 18mins

INGREDIENTS

- 1 - package DODO crabsticks
- 2 - tsp oil
- Flavoring powder

INSTRUCTIONS

1. Establish your air-fryer to 160 levels and also pre-heat for 5 mins.

2. Damage the crab sticks length-wise as well as shred right into littler, also items.

3. Ensure not to recompense the ruining. 1.5 to 2cm size would certainly be respectable.

4. To achieve an even more also size you can unfold each crab stick, layer one over the various other and also reduced in a similar way.

5. Place in a dish and also spray oil over. Toss well to combine.

6. Air-fry for 12 mins till fantastic dark tinted. No engaging factor to stock a solitary layer so lehceh.

7. Open up home plate at normal periods and also make use of a number of tongs to toss with the objective that they will certainly prepare consistently.

8. Sprinkle daintily with your choice of seasoning on the off possibility that you such as.

Baked Zucchini French Fries

Servings: 6
Time: Preparation Time: 10mins, Prepare Time: 20mins

INGREDIENTS

3 - tool zucchini cut right into sticks
2 - big egg white

1/2 - mug skilled bread crumbs
2 - tablespoon grated Parmesan cheese
cooking spray
1/4 - tsp garlic powder
salt & pepper to preference

DIRECTIONS

1. Preheat cooktop to 425â °
. 2. Identify an air conditioning shelf inside a preparing sheet and also layer shelf with a food preparation dash; deposited.
3. In a little dish, defeat egg whites as well as period with salt as well as pepper.
4. In an additional dish, location breadcrumbs, garlic powder, and also cheddar and also mix well.
5. Dunk zucchini penetrates eggs after that right into bread scrap and also cheddar mix, a pair at any type of provided minute.
6. Find the breaded zucchini in a singular layer onto the air conditioning shelf as well as shower even more cooking dash ahead.
7. Warm at 425â ° for around 15-20 mins, or up until dazzling dark tinted.
8. Existing with Cattle ranch or Marinara sauce for diving.

Cajun Curly French Fries

Servings: 2
Time: Preparation Time: 40mins, Prepare Time: 15mins

INGREDIENTS

- 2 - big cooking potatoes
- 1 - tbsp olive oil
- 2 - tbsps Cajun spices mix
- 1 - tsp garlic powder
- Salt and also pepper to preference

DIRECTIONS

1. Use your spiralizer to spiralizer the potatoes as suggested by headings.

2. You should have a bumpy rotisserie reducing side for this.
3. Soak up the potatoes water for thirty minutes.
4. Network the water and also obtain completely dry the potatoes. Toss them with oil as well as your flavorings.
5. These potatoes can take in a lots of flavor, so do not hesitate to period kindly.
6. Pre-heat your air fryer to 390 levels F as well as include fifty percent of the potatoes to the pet crate.
7. Prepare for 10-15 mins accumulation, mixing the dog crate a number of times amidst food preparation up until they are to your preferred quality.
8. Get rid of and also do also for the remainder of the potatoes.
9. Value.

Pork & 3 Cheese Two Times

Baked Potatoes

Servings:
Time: Preparation Time: 15mins, Prepare Time: 15mins

INGREDIENTS

- 4 - tool baker potatoes
- 1/2 - c. sour lotion
- 3/4 - c. milk
- 2/3c. white cheddar grated
- 1/2 c. grated Parmesan
- 1/4 - tsp. garlic salt
- 1 1/2 c. diced pork
- 8 - oz. sharp Cheddar shredded
- 1/3c. environment-friendly onion sliced

DIRECTIONS

1. Stab every potato 2 inches deep with a blade numerous times. Microwave the potatoes for 5 mins.

2. Making use of a griddle handwear cover to protect your hand from the warm potato, reduced them fifty-fifty the lengthy method and also dig the cells, leaving a 1/4 inch of potato on the brink.

3. In a little dish, extra pound the potatoes as well as consist of the rough lotion, Parmesan, White Cheddar, and also garlic salt.

4. Load the potato skins with the battered potato mix and also using the rear of a spoon, framework a divot between.

5. Fill up every divot with 3 Tbsps of diced pork.

6. Arrange 4 potato skins in a little Air-fryer or 8 out of an XL Air-fryer.

7. Warm at 300 ° in the Air-fryer for 8 mins. Leading with ruined cheddar as well as prepare an added 2 mins.

8. Offer completed with diced environment-friendly onions.

Spinach Artichoke White Pizza

Servings: 2
Time: Preparation Time: 20mins, Prepare Time: 15mins

INGREDIENTS

- olive oil
- 3 - mugs fresh spinach
- 2 - cloves garlic
- 6- to 8-ounce pizza dough round
- 1/2 - mug mozzarella cheese
- 1/4 - mug grated Fontina cheese
- 1/4 - mug artichoke hearts
- 2 - tsp grated Parmesan cheese
- 1/4 - tsp dried out oregano
- salt and also ground black pepper

DIRECTIONS

1. Heat the oil in a tool sauté recipe at the stovetop.

2. Consist of the spinach and also a big component of the minced garlic to the meal as well as sauté for a couple of mins, till the spinach has actually shriveled.

3. Get rid of the sautéed spinach from the container as well as positioned it apart.

4. Pre-warmness the air fryer to 390°F.

5. Eliminate a little light weight aluminum foil an equivalent dimension as the base of the air fryer bushel.

6. Brush the aluminum foil float with olive oil. Forming the batter right into a circle and also see it over the aluminum foil.

7. Anchor the batter via penetrating it a couple of times with a fork.

8. Brush the combination naturally with olive oil and also pass it right into the air fryer cage with the aluminum foil under.

9. Air-broil the evident pizza accumulation for 6mins.

10. Transform the mix over, leave the light weight aluminum foil and also brush again with olive oil, air-broil for an additional 4 mins.

11. Spray the Parmesan cheddar and also dried out oregano on peak as well as shower with olive oil.

12. Period to taste with salt as well as crisp flooring dark pepper.

Crispy Roasted Onion Potatoes

Servings: 3
Time: Preparation Time: 5mins, Prepare Time: 20mins

INGREDIENTS

- 2 - pound. infant red potatoes
- 2 - Tablespoon. olive oil
- 1 - envelope Lipton onion soup mix

DIRECTIONS

1. Quarter the potatoes as well as toss them in the olive oil in a tool dish.

2. Consist of the onion soup mix as well as blend up until each of the potatoes is quite covered.

3. Include the potatoes to the Air-fryer container and also chef at 390 ° for 17-20 mins, mixing the potatoes component of the means via.

Mac and Cheese Balls

Servings: 8
Time: Preparation Time: 40mins, Prepare Time: 2hrs 12mins

Ingredients

- 1 - pound Macaroni
- 2 - 8 oz Colby Jack cheese
- 4 - jalapenos diced
- 1 1/4 - mug Whole Milk
- 1/2 - mug Flour
- 1/4 - mug Butter
- 2 - Eggs
- 3 - mug Panko
- Salt & Pepper to taste

Directions

1. For Air Fryer Mac as well as Cheese Balls. Bubble macaroni up until fragile

2. Shred your Colby as well as Jack cheddar as well as deposited.

3. Shakers your jalapeños as well as readied to the side

4. In a big container, over tool heat soften your spread

5. Consist of flour and also mix till signed up with as well as its a light dark tinted shielding.

6. Consist of some whole milk as well as thrill till thick.

7. Include your cheddar one glass at any type of provided minute. Mix up until cheddar is entirely liquified as well as smooth.

8. Consist of the macaroni as well as jalapenos and also mix up until significantly covered.

9. Consist of salt as well as pepper.

10. Currently position your macaroni and also cheddar in an area as well as location it in your refrigerator. Cooler for 60 mins.

11. Line a preparing sheet with product paper.

12. Framework your macaroni as well as cheddar right into 1 ″ spheres as well as area on your container.

13. An area in colder for 60 mins.

14. In a tool determined dish defeated the eggs and also consist of 1/4 container milk in a dish.

15. Dive spheres right into egg laundry then been available in the panko. Emphasize to layer entirely.

16. Warmth your Air Fryer to 380' as well as prepare for 12 mins.

Nourishment Info: Calories 570g, Fat 35g, CarbS 32g, Sugars 1g, Healthy Protein 29g

3 Ingredient Fried Catfish

Servings: 4
Time: Preparation Time: 15mins, Prepare Time: 1hr 5mins

Ingredients

- 4 - catfish fillets
- 1/4 - mug experienced fish fry I made use of Louisiana
- 1 - tablespoon olive oil
- 1 - tablespoon cut parsley optional

Directions

1. Preheat Air Fryer to 400 levels.

2. Clean the catfish and also rub completely dry.

3. Put the fish rotisserie flavor in a big Ziploc pack.

4. Include the catfish to the sack, every one consequently. Seal the pack as well as shake. Assurance the entire filet is covered with flavor.

5. Dash olive oil on the acme of each filet.

6. Find the filet airborne Fryer bushel. Close and also prepare for 10 mins.

7. Turn the fish. Prepare for an additional 10 mins.

8. Prepare for an additional 2-3 mins or up until needed quality.

9. Leading with parsley.

Nourishment Details: Calories 460g, Fat 19g, CarbS 52g, Sugars 1g, Healthy Protein 19g

Keto Shrimp Scampi

Servings: 4
Time: Preparation Time: 5mins, Prepare Time: 10mins

Ingredients

- 4 - tbsps butter
- 1 - tbsp lemon juice
- 1 - tbsp diced garlic
- 2 - tsps red pepper flakes
- 1 - tbsp cut chives
- 1 - tbsp diced basil fallen leaves
- 2 - tbsps poultry supply
- 1 - pound thawed shrimp

Directions

1. Transform your air fryer to 330F. Find a 6 x 3 steel meal in it and also allow the cooktop to start warming up while you construct your correctings.

2. Identify the margarine, garlic, and also red pepper chips right into the warm 6-inch frying pan.

3. Allow it to prepare for 2 mins, mixing when, till the spread has actually softened.

4. This is things that imbues garlic right into the margarine, which is the important things that makes every little thing preference so terrific.

5. Open up the air fryer, include all dealings with to the container in the demand videotaped, blending gently.

6. Enable shrimp to prepare for 5 mins, blending when. Currently, the margarine should certainly be significantly softened and also liquid, cleaning the shrimp in spiced benefits.

7. Mix terrific, leave the 6-inch frying pan using silicone handwear covers as well as allow it relax for 1 min on the counter.

8. You're doing this with the objective that you allow the shrimp chef in the remaining heat, rather than allowing it by the way overcook as well as obtain rubbery.

9. Mix towards the min's end. The shrimp should be throughout prepared currently.

10. Sprinkle additional brand-new basil leaves as well as value.

Nutrition: Calories 660g, Fat 43g, CarbS 45g, Sugars 1g, Healthy Protein 26g

Parmesan Shrimp

Servings: 4
Time: Preparation Time: 10mins, Prepare Time: 15mins

Ingredients

- 2 - extra pounds big prepared shrimp
- 4 - cloves garlic
- 2/3 - mug parmesan cheese
- 1 - tsp pepper
- 1/2 - tsp oregano
- 1 - tsp basil
- 1 - tsp onion powder
- 2 - tbsps olive oil
- Lemon

Directions

1. In a huge dish, becomes part of garlic, parmesan cheddar, pepper, oregano, basil, onion powder, as well as olive oil?
2. Tenderly toss shrimp in combination up until equitably covered.
3. Sprinkle air fryer box with non-stick bathe and also notification shrimp inside the dog crate.
4. Prepare at 350 degrees for 8-10 mins or up until flavor on shrimp is caramelized.
5. Squash the lemon over the shrimp prior to offering.

Nutrition: Calories 82.1 g, Fat 1.6 g, Carbs 3.2 g, Sugars 0.8 g, Healthy protein 12.2 g.

Fried Louisiana Shrimp with Remoulade Sauce

Servings: 4.
Time: Preparation Time: 20mins, Prepare Time: 10mins.

Ingredients

- 1 - extra pound shrimp.
- 1/2 - mug Louisiana Fish Fry.
- 1/4 - mug buttermilk.
- 4 - French bread sub rolls.
- 2 - mugs shredded lettuce.
- 8 - tomato pieces.
- 1 - tsp Creole Flavoring.
- 1 - tsp butter optional.

Remoulade Sauce.

- 1/2 - mug mayo.
- 1 - tsp diced garlic.
- 1/2 - lemon juice of.
- 1 - tsp Worcestershire.
- 1/2 - tsp Creole Flavoring.
- 1 - tsp Dijon mustard.
- 1 - tsp warm sauce.
- 1 - environment-friendly onion.

Directions

1. Combine lots of people of the mendings in a little bit dish. Cool prior to offering also as the shrimp cooks.
2. Put the buttermilk in a dish. Dunk each of the shrimp inside the buttermilk.
3. Find the shrimp in a Ziploc sack and also in the ice upper body to marinade. Season for something like half-hour.
4. Include the fish rotisserie to a dish. Remove the shrimp from the packs and also dive every right into the fish rotisserie.
5. Include the shrimp to Air Fryer box.
6. Preheat Air Fryer to 400 phases.
7. Bath the shrimp with olive oil. Attempt not to shower straight at the shrimp.
8. Prepare for an added 5 mins or till fresh.
9. Preheat griddle to 325 degrees. Find the decrease bread on a sheet frying pan.
10. Allow the bread to salute for 2 or 3 mins.
11. Making use of a food preparation brush, spread out the margarine over all-time low of the French bread.
12. Accumulate the po young person. Spread out the remoulade sauce at the French bread.
13. Consist of the cut tomato and also lettuce, and also later the shrimp.

Nutrition: Calories 213.8 g, Fat 7.3 g, Carbs 33.4 g, Sugars 12.2 g, Healthy protein 3.7 g.

Hasselback Potatoes

Servings: 4.
Time: Preparation Time: 15mins, Prepare Time: 30mins.

Ingredients

- 4 -potatoes.
- Olive oil, as required.
- Bacon little bits.
- Shredded cheese.

Directions

1. Contingent upon your disposition, either strip the potatoes or leave the skins on.
2. When it comes to using significant potatoes, reduced them down the center. Cut reduces along the potatoes around 1/4-inch apart as well as around 3/8-inch from the base of the potato.
3. Pre-heat the air fryer to 355 ° F (180 ° C).
4. Naturally clean the potatoes with olive oil and also prepare them in your air fryer for 15 mins.
5. After they have actually prepared for 15 mins, comb them once again with oil as well as continue food preparation for an added 15 mins or up until or up until they are prepared with.

Nutrition: Calories 243.2 g, Fat 11.5 g, Carbs 31g, Sugars 1.4 g, Healthy protein 5.3 g.

Chunky Crab Cake

Servings: 8
Time: Preparation Time: 15mins, Prepare Time: 20mins

Ingredients

- 2 - huge eggs
- 2 - tbsps mayo
- 1 - tsp Dijon mustard
- 1 - tsp Worcestershire sauce
- 1 1/2 - tsp Old Bay spices
- Fresh pepper to preference
- 1/4 - mug carefully sliced environment-friendly onion
- 1 - extra pound swelling crab meat
- 1/3 to 1/2 - mug panko

Directions

1. Sign up with the egg, mayo, Dijon mustard, Worcestershire, Old Bay in a tool dish and also mix well. Consist of the carefully hacked eco-friendly onion to the mayo mix and also mix naturally.
2. Include the crab to the mayo mix up until all combined. Include the panko to the crab/mayonnaise incorporate as well as overlay till just signed up with, being conscious so as not to over mix maintaining the crab swellings perfect.
3. Spread out the crab mix as well as detect in the colder for about 60 mins.
4. Forming right into around 8 crab cakes of 1 inch thick; emphasize to not load the cakes as well strongly.
5. Pre-heat the air-fryer to 350F. When the air-fryer attains the optimal temperature level, naturally location 4 crab cakes right into the container as well as readied to air sear for 10 mins, the crab cake should certainly be established as well as with a light hull. Emphasize to turn the crab cakes adhering to 5 mins to attain regardless of food preparation.
6. Whenever prepared, tenderly exchange to a plate. Existing with lemon wedges.

Nutrition: Calories 129.2 g, Fat 2.5 g, Carbs 8.1 g, Sugars 1.6 g, Healthy protein 17.1 g.

Perfect Steak

Servings: 2.
Time: Preparation Time: 20mins, Prepare Time: 20mins.

Ingredients

- 28 - oz Ribeye steak.
- salt.
- newly fractured black pepper.
- olive oil.
- Garlic Butter.
- 1 - stick saltless butter softened.

- 2 - Tablespoon fresh parsley cut.
- 2 - tsp garlic diced.
- 1 - tsp Worcestershire Sauce.
- 1/2 - tsp salt.

Directions

1. Strategy Garlic Butter by mixing spread, parsley garlic, Worcestershire sauce, as well as salt till entirely signed up with.

2. Area in product paper as well as layer right into a log. Cool till prepared to use.

3. Get rid of steak from the colder and also allow to rest at area temperature level for 20 mins.

4. Massage a smidgen of olive oil on both sides of the steak and also period with salt as well as crisply busted dark pepper.

5. Oil your Air Fryer bushel by combing a little of oil on the dog crate. Preheat Air Fryer to 400 levels Fahrenheit.

6. When preheated, location steaks in air fryer as well as chef for 12 mins, turning component of the means via.

7. Get rid of from air fryer as well as allow to relax for 5 mins. Leading with garlic spread.

Nutrition: Calories 170.1 g, Fat 3g, Carbs 21g, Sugars 0.2 g, Healthy protein 14g.

Quick Mix Jamaican Hen

Meatballs

Servings: 10.
Time: Preparation Time: 5mins, Prepare Time: 15mins.

Ingredients

- Blender or food processor.
- 2 - Hen Breasts.
- 1 - Big Onion peeled off and also diced.
- 2 - Tablespoon Honey.
- 3 - Tablespoon Soy Sauce.
- 1 - Tsp Chilli Powder.

- 1 - Tablespoon Thyme.
- 1 - Tablespoon Basil.
- 1 - Tablespoon Cumin.
- 1 - Tablespoon Mustard Powder.
- 2 - Tsp Jerk Paste optional.
- Salt & Pepper.

Directions

1. Identify the hen right into the blender or food processor and also mix up until it appears like poultry dice.

2. Identify the onion right into the blender or food processor also and also blend well.

3. Consist of all the Jamaican spices as well as mix for the 3rd time.

4. Open your mixer as well as make 10 average gauged meatballs.

5. Find them on a preparing floor covering inside your air fryer as well as prepare them for 15 mins on 180c.

6. When they're established place them on sticks, then spoon over them a section of the sauce that is still around the sides of your blender or food processor for conclusive sticky meatballs taste feeling.

7. Sprinkle with crisp natural herbs as well as offer.

Nutrition: Calories 80g, Fat 1g, Carbs 5g, Sugars 4g, Healthy Protein 10g.

Pork Tenderloin with Bell Pepper

Servings: 2.
Time: Preparation Time: 10mins, Prepare Time: 15mins.

Ingredients

- 1 - red or yellow bell pepper, in slim strips.
- 1 - red onion, in slim pieces.
- 2 - tsps Provençal natural herbs.
- Newly ground black pepper.
- 1 - tbsp olive oil.
- 1 - pork tenderloin - 300 g.

- 1/2 - tbsp mustard.
- Round 15 centimeters stove meal.

Directions
1. Pre-heat the air-fryer to 200 ° C.
2. In the recipe, mix the ringer pepper strips with the onion, the Provençal natural herbs, as well as some salt and also pepper to preference.
3. Include 1/2 tbsp olive oil to the mix.
4. Meagerly layer the items with olive oil and also detect them upstanding in the recipe over the pepper mix.
5. Find the dish in the container and also glide the bushel right into the air-fryer.
6. Establish the clock to 15 mins as well as dish the meat and also the veggies.
7. Transform the meat and also mix the peppers component of the means via the preparation time.
8. Fascinating with pureed potatoes and also a crisp plate of combined environment-friendlies.

Nutrition: Calories 200g, Fat 12g, Carbs 2g, Sugars 0.4 g, Healthy protein 20g.

General Tso's Chicken

Servings: 4.
Time: Preparation Time: 10mins, Prepare Time: 25mins.

Ingredients
- 1.5-2 pounds poultry upper legs.
- 1/3 - mug potato starch.
- 1 - Tablespoon grease.
- 6 - dried out red chillies.
- 3 - environment-friendly onions.
- 2 - tsp garlic.
- 1 - tsp ginger.
- 3/4 - mug brownish sugar.
- 1/2 - mug poultry brew.
- 1/2 - mug soy sauce.
- 2 - Tablespoon rice vinegar.

- 1 - tsp sesame oil.
- 1 - pinch of salt.
- 2 - tsp corn starch.
- 1/4 - mug water.

Directions
1. Establish Air Fryer to 400 levels Fahrenheit. Cover hen upper legs with potato starch making certain all items are totally protected.
2. Usage tongs to place poultry items in Air Fryer bushel. Prepare poultry items for 20-25 mins up until fresh, drinking container like clockwork.
3. In the meanwhile, strategy sauce by warming up grease in a frying pan over medium-high heat.
4. When warm, consist of eco-friendly onions, dried out chilies, garlic, and also ginger as well as sautéed food for around 1 min till chilies brighten in shielding as well as onions have actually mollified.
5. Consist of dark tinted sugar, hen soup, soy sauce, rice vinegar, sesame oil, and also a capture of salt to the frying pan and also mix.
6. Warmth to the factor of steaming as well as chef for around 3 mins.
7. When hen in air fryer is done, contribute to sauce as well as mix in.
8. Make a thickener by blending 2 tsps of corn starch in 1/4 container infection water.
9. Mix right into gurgling sauce and also allow to prepare for around 1 min, up until sauce has actually enlarged.
10. Existing with rice as well as veggie as well as Enjoy.

Nutrition: Calories 115g, Fat 8.8 g, Carbs 3.1 g, Sugars 0.3 g, Healthy protein 5.8 g.

Crispy Low-Fat Fried Chicken

Serving: 6

Time: Preparation Time: 1hr 5mins, Prepare
Time: 30mins

Ingredients
- 1 - whole chicken
- 2 - mugs buttermilk
- 1-- tbs. warm sauce
- 1 - mug Kentucky Bit flour
- oil for splashing

Directions
1. Mix buttermilk and warm sauce.
2. Detect hen in a significant dish and pour the buttermilk blend over it. Cool for 60 mins.
3. Place the ready flour either in a substantial bowl or plastic sack. Channel poultry as well as dig in the flour.
4. Find chicken obvious all over fryer pet crate; shower with oil and also chef at 380 levels F for 30 minutes, transforming the chicken component of the means through the chef time and also sprinkling the transformed side with oil.

Nutrition: Calories 350g, Fat 20g, Carbs 15g, Sugars 2g, Healthy Protein 20g

Finest Old Fashioned Meatloaf

Serving: 4
Time: Prep Time: 10mins, Cook Time: 45mins

Ingredients
- 2 1/2 - lbs. combination of sliced beef
- 2 - eggs
- bread crumbs regarding 3/4 to 1 cup
- 1/2 - cup sliced fresh parsley
- 1 - little carrot
- 1 - finely cut shallot
- 1 1/2 - tbs. catsup
- 1/2 - tbs. Worcestershire sauce
- 2 - tsp. Dijon mustard
- salt and also pepper to preference
- 8 - oz. can of tomato sauce
- 1 1/2 - cup frozen peas

Directions
1. Pre-heat the air fryer to 330 degrees.
2. Sprinkle the air fryer cage with food preparation shower, put the raw meatloaf right into the container.
3. Give a little sprinkle to the acme of the meat part and also prepare at 330 for 14 mins.
4. check to ensure it's cooking and also searing legitimately. Use a meat thermostat to look for doneness. My 2 1/2 pound. meatloaf cooks an aggregate of 25 to half an hour.
5. While the meatloaf if cooking, consist of the tomato sauce and also solidified peas in a microwave spare recipe and also warmth up when the meat portion has just 2 mins left to cook.
6. Leave the cooked meat part and place on a plate. Pour the warmed up tomato sauce and also peas over the meat part and also offer.

Nutrition: Calories 1760g, Fat 122g, Carbs 88g, Sugars 21g, Protein 70g

Cajun Salmon

Serving: 6
Time: Prep Time: 10mins, Prepare Time: 15mins

Ingredients
- 1 - piece fresh salmon fillet
- Cajun seasoning
- A light spray of sugar
- Juice from a quarter of lemon

Directions

1. Pre-heat your air-fryer to 180C. For the Philips air-fryer, the orange light will go out to show that the temperature level has been involved.

2. For different brands, ordinarily, simply pre-heat for 5 minutes.

3. Tidy your salmon and also pat dry. In a plate, spray Cajun seasoning all ended up and also ensure all sides are covered.

4. You don't require excessively. In case you prefer a little sweet taste, include a light scattering of sugar.

5. NO flavoring time needed.

6. For a salmon filet around 3/4 of an inch thick, air-fry for 7 mins, skin side up on the bbq meal.

7. Offer promptly with a press of lemon.

Nutrition: Calories 240g, Fat 5g, Carbs 39g, Sugars 3g, Protein 8g

Sticky BBQ Pork Strips

Servings: 2
Time: Preparation Time: 2hrs 5mins, Cook Time: 16mins

Ingredients
- 6-- pc Pork Loin Chops
- 1 - tsp Balsamic Vinegar
- 2 - tablespoon Soy Sauce
- 2 - tablespoon Honey
- 1 - clove Garlic
- 1/4 - tsp Ground Ginger
- Newly Ground Pepper

Directions
1. Utilize a meat tenderizer to work the slashes at that point season with some ground brand-new pepper.

2. To establish the marinade, pour the balsamic vinegar, soy sauce, and nectar right into a dish.

3. Consist of lowered garlic and ground ginger right into the sauce blend. Mix to blend it well as well as put aside.

4. Join pork slashes with the marinate mix and desert it to season for 2 hours or medium-term.

5. Preheat the Air-fryer at 180 ° C for 5 mins.

6. Air-Fry the cleaves in the preparing plate together with the sauce juice for 5 to 8 mins on each side until it prepared completely and also transformed great darker.

7. When it is cooked, reduced the meat into strips or you can offer it as slashes.

Nutrition: Calories 240g, Fat 15g, Carbs 1.5 g, Sugars 1g, Healthy Protein 27g

Chinese Mongolian Beef

Servings: 4
Time: Prep Time: 20mins, Cook Time: 20mins

Ingredients

Meat
- 1 - Lb Flank Steak
- 1/4 - Cup Corn Starch

Sauce
- 2 - Tsp Grease
- 1/2 - Tsp Ginger
- 0.4 oz. Soy Sauce
- 1 - Tablespoon Minced Garlic
- 1/2 - Cup Water
- 3/4 - Cup Brown Sugar Packed

Extras
- Prepared Rice
- Environment-friendly Beans
- Environment-friendly Onions

INSTRUCTIONS
1. Meagerly reduce the steak in lengthy items, at that point coat with the corn starch.

2. Spot in the Air Fryer and also prepare on 390 * for 10 mins on each side.

3. While the steak concocts, heat up all sauce repairing in a tool measured pot on medium-high heat.

4. Blend the mendings with each other till it reaches a reduced bubble.

5. When both the steak and also sauce are cooked, position the steak in a dish with the sauce as well as let it soak up for around 5-10 mins.

6. At the point when prepared to serve, make use of tongs to evacuate the steak and let the wealth sauce trickle off.

7. Spot steak on prepared rice as well as environment-friendly beans, leading with extra sauce on the off possibility that you lean toward.

Nutrition: Calories 160g, Fat 10g, Carbs 1g, Sugars 4g, Protein 18g

Italian Meatball Air Fryer Style

Serving: 24
Time: Preparation Time: 8mins, Cook Time: 15mins

INGREDIENTS

- 2 - pounds. of hamburger
- 2 - big eggs
- 1/4 - cup bread crumbs
- 1/4 - cup chopped fresh parsley
- 1 - tsp. dried oregano
- 1/4 - cup grated parmigiano reggiano
- 1 - tiny clove garlic
- salt and also pepper to preference
- 1 - tsp. light oil dabbed on a paper towel

DIRECTIONS

1. Identify the meat and also every one of the fixings in a comprehensive mixing bowl.

2. Incorporate each of the correctings together with your arms.

3. Mix the dealings with just till every little thing is throughout combined.

4. Gather up a little bit handful of meat as well as can be found in the palm of your hand on your finest length meatball.

5. Or however, you may take advantage of a handle scoop to be able to find up with even length meatballs.

6. Set up the Air Fryer as in maintaining with producer directions.

7. Prepare them at 350 rates for 10-13mins till delicately sautéed.

8. Turn them a range and cook some other four-5mins. Evacuate to a plate while prepared.

9. Whenever arranged, position them into the tomato sauce to hold cooking.

10. Present along with your most cherished pasta.

Nourishment Details: Calories 284g, Fat 18g, Carbs 2g, Sugars 5g, Protein 30g

Air Fryer Tangy Bbq Poultry

Servings: 2
Time: Prep Time: 20mins, Cook Time: 45mins

ACTIVE INGREDIENTS

- 5 - tbsps of balsamic vinegar
- 1/4 - cup of brownish sugar
- 3 - tbsps of soy sauce
- 3 - tbsps of olive oil
- 3 - tbsps of Dijon mustard
- 4 - Boneless Skinless Chicken Bust

DIRECTIONS

1. Mix most of the sauce repairings in a dish, combination nicely.

2. Then include your hen, as well as allow sauce for around thirty minutes.

3. Spot the chook properly at the rack crucial all around a fryer.

4. Prepare for 15mins at 380 stages Fahrenheit.

Nutrition Information: Calories 320g, Fat 8g, Carbs 4g, Sugars 2g, Healthy Protein 68g

Air Fryer Tasty Fish

Serving: 6
Time: Prep Time: 35mins, Cook Time: 25mins

INGREDIENTS
- Four tbsps of vegetable oil
- 100grams - of breadcrumbs
- 1 - blended egg
- 4 - fish fillets
- 1 - lemon

DIRECTIONS
1. Preheat the air fryer to 180 levels Celsius.
2. Blend both the oil and also 100 grams of breadcrumbs in a bowl. Keep on mixing it up until the blend turns totally free as well as breakable.
3. Plunge the fish filets into the egg at that point get rid of any kind of egg buildup.
4. Presently plunge the fish filets in the scrap mix, guaranteeing that the fish is equally and altogether protected with the breadcrumbs and also oil.
5. Presently naturally position the fish visible all over the fryer, food preparation it for around 12 minutes.
6. You will realize that the fish is prepared once it has fantastic darker shielding and also looks crispy.
7. The moment may fluctuate, contingent upon exactly how thick your fish is.
8. So you must identify the condition of it at routine periods to abstain from overcooking.
9. When the fish is prepared, allow it to cool and offer it with lemon and most liked sides and repairings. Value

Nutrition Information: Calories 226.7 g, Fat 10.7 g, Carbs 14.2 g, Sugars 4.6 g, Healthy protein 19.2 g.

Air Fryer Spicy Chicken Empanadas

Servings: 3.
Time: Preparation Time: mins25, Chef Time: 20mins.

INGREDIENTS.
- 1 - box of Cooled Pie Crust.
- 2 - rolls.
- 1 - mug shredded rotisserie Poultry.
- 1/2 - mug shredded Cheddar Cheese.
- 1/4 - mug chopped Environment-friendly Onion.
- 1/2 - cup chopped Cilantro.
- 2 - sliced Jalapeno.
- 1/2 - tsp Garlic Powder.
- 1/2 - tsp ground Cumin.
- 2 - tsp Hot Sauce.
- Salt as well as pepper to taste.
- Egg.
- 1/2 - mug Sour Cream.
- 1 - tsp chopped Environment-friendly Onion/Scallion.
- 1/2 - mug chopped Cilantro.
- 1/4 - tsp Chili pepper.
- 1/4 - tsp smoked Paprika.
- Salt to taste.

DIRECTIONS.
1. In a large bowl, combine ruined poultry, cheddar, reduced green onions, jalapeno and also cilantro, garlic powder, ground cumin, hot sauce, and salt and pepper.
2. Unfold the pie blend onto a well-rounded floured surface. Utilizing a 5-inch round intermediary, cut out nevertheless several circles as could sensibly be expected.

3. Using a relocating pin, disclose the items as well as keep getting rid of hovers until the battery goes out.

4. Rework the equal with the other pie dough. Spoon around 1 tbsp of the intense poultry filling into the center of batter.

5. Overlap the batter fifty-fifty over the dental filling, forming a fifty percent circle, then make use of the fingers to tenderly press and also secure the edges.

6. Utilize a fork to wrinkle the edges together.

7. Brush each empanada with the egg wash.

8. Air-fry the empanadas at 400 F for 10 mins.

9. Serve hot with Cilantro-Scallion Dipping Sauce.

Nutrition Details: Calories 366.5 g, Fat 3.9 g, Carbs 26.4 g, Sugars 7.2 g, Protein 56.8g.

Chicken Kabobs

Serving: 2.
Time: Prep Time: 15mins, Prepare Time: 15mins.

INGREDIENTS.

- 1/3 - cup Honey.
- 1/3 - cup Soy sauce.
- Salt.
- Pepper cut into little squares.
- Sesame.
- 6 - Mushrooms chop in half.
- 3 - Bell peppers.
- Oil a few spray.
- 2 - Chicken busts diced.

DIRECTIONS

1. Shakers 2 poultry breasts into 3D squares include a place of pepper, salt and few showers of oil.

2. Consist of 1/3 step of nectar as well as 1/3 procedure of sauce soy, incorporate each well. Include some sesame seeds as well as mix well.

3. Clean some wood sticks start placing in peppers, poultries and also mushroom pieces onto the sticks.

4. Pre-heat air-fryer at 170 ° C/338 ° F, coat all the poultry shish kebabs with the combined sauce.

5. Concern all the poultry kabobs into the air-fryer bin, chef under 170 ° C/338 ° F for 15mins-20mins, prepared to offer.

Nourishment Details: Calories 188g, Fat 4g, Carbs 12g, Sugar 2.3 g, Healthy protein 25g.

Air Fryer Ranch Chicken Tenders

Servings: 4.
Time: Prep Time: 5mins, Cook Time: 15mins.

ACTIVE INGREDIENTS.

- 8 - chicken tenders.
- canola or non-fat food preparation spray.

For the Dredge Terminal:

- 1 - cup panko breadcrumbs.
- 1 - egg.
- 2 - tbsps of water.

For the Ranch Chicken Flavoring:

- 1/2 - tsp Salt.
- 1 - teaspoon pepper.
- 1/2 - tsp Garlic powder.
- 1/2 - tsp Onion powder.
- 1/4 - tsp Paprika.
- 1 - tsp Dried parsley.

DIRECTIONS

1. Pre-heat the Air Fryer. Warm the air fryer via establishing it to 400 rates F for 5mins.

2. Allow it to preserve walking without nutrients in the container.

3. Blend the water and also egg jointly in a superficial bowl.

4. Establish the Ranch Seasoning. In a little bowl, settle each of the seasonings for the farm flavor.

5. Period the Poultry. Sprinkle the poultry strips with the farm flavor, turning to layer the two sides.

6. Dig the hen. Dunk chicken strips into the egg laundry and after that press it right into the panko.

7. Burden the Fryer Basket. Spot the breaded tenders right into the broil dog crate. Rehash with staying tenders.

8. Burn the Hen. Find the Fry Basket into the Power Air Fryer XL.

9. Sprinkle a light layer of canola oil of non-fat food preparation shower over the panko.

10. Want to the Fried Poultry Symbol. Press the Power Button.

Nutritional Info: Calories 197g, Fat 4g, Carbs 12g, Sugar 2g, Healthy Protein 25g.

Chicken Fajita Rollups

Servings: 4
Time: Preparation Time: 25mins, Prepare Time: 35mins

ACTIVE INGREDIENTS

- 3 - hen busts
- 1/2 - of a huge Red Bell Pepper
- 1/2 - of a big eco-friendly bell pepper
- 1/2 - of a big yellow bell pepper
- 1/2 - big red onion cut
- 2 - tsps paprika
- 1 - tsp garlic powder
- 1 - tsp cumin powder
- 1/2 - tsp Chili pepper
- 1/2 - tsp Mexican Oregano
- Salt & Pepper to Preference

- Olive Oil or spray haze
- toothpicks to safeguard the roll-ups

DIRECTIONS

1. Mix the tastes in a little dish as well as maintain apart.

2. When it comes to making use of hen breasts, reduced them the lengthy means right into 2 also cuts.

3. Place each breast fifty percent or cutlet in between worldly paper as well as immovably extra pound the poultry using a frustrating write-up, comparable to the base of an actors iron container, relocating the pin.

4. Kindly period both sides of each straightened out hen cutlet with the prepared taste rub.

5. Area 6 sections of chile pepper and also a number of onion cuts on one side of the hen. Go up securely as well as protect with toothpicks.

6. Spray any type of added taste rub over the poultry goes up. Area 3 poultry rollups in the gently lubed air fryer bushel.

7. Daintily bath the roll-ups with oil dash or haze Air-fryer at 400 F for 12 mins. Rehash with the complying with lot.

8. Offer warm with a plate of blended eco-friendlies of choice for a divine reduced carbohydrate dinner.

Nourishment Details: Calories 260g, Fat 5g, Carbs 6g, Sugars 2g, Healthy Protein 44g

Bourbon Bacon Hamburger

Servings: 2
Time: Preparation Time: 15mins, Prepare Time: 20mins

INGREDIENTS

- 1 - tbsp bourbon
- 2 - tbsps brownish sugar

- 3 - strips maple bacon
- 3/4 - extra pound hamburger
- 1 - tbsp diced onion
- 2 - tbsps BARBEQUE sauce
- 1/2 - tsp salt
- newly ground black pepper
- 2 - pieces Colby Jack cheese
- 2 - Kaiser rolls
- lettuce and also tomato

Zesty Hamburger Sauce:
- 2 - tbsps BARBEQUE sauce
- 2 - tbsps mayo
- 1/4 - tsp ground paprika
- newly ground black pepper

GUIDELINES

1.Pre-warmness the air fryer to 390°F and also clear a little water right into all-time low of the air fryer cabinet.

2. Sign up with the bourbon as well as dark tinted sugar in a touch dish.

3. Find the bacon strips terrific all rounded fryer container and also brush with the darkish-colored sugar mix.

4. Sign up with the flooring meat, onion, BARBEQUE sauce, salt and also pepper in a considerable dish.

5. Settle definitely along with your arms and also create the beef right into 2 patties.

6. Exchange the hamburger patties to the air fryer container and also air-broil the hamburgers at 370°F for 15 to twenty mins, section upon just how you like your hamburger prepared.

7. Turn the hamburgers over a component of the way using the food preparation approach.

8. While the hamburgers are air-fricasseeing, make the hamburger sauce using signing up with the BARBEQUE sauce, mayo, paprika, as well as crisply flooring darkish pepper to taste in a dish.

9. At the aspect when the hamburgers are prepared for your taking pleasure in, leading each patty with a cut of Colby Jack cheddar as well as air-broil for an added 2nd, simply to liquify the cheddar. Spread out the sauce inside the Kaiser activities, an area the hamburgers on the actions, peak with the scotch bacon, lettuce and also tomato, and also regard.

Nourishment Info: Calories 290g, Fat 11g, Carbs 5g, Sugars 2g, Healthy Protein 41g

Garlic Parmesan Roasted Potatoes

Servings 6
Time: Preparation Time: 20mins, Prepare Time: 20mins

ACTIVE INGREDIENTS
- 1/2 -tsp basil
- 5 -cloves garlic
- 1/2 -tsp oregano
- 2 -tbsps parsley leaves
- 3 -extra pounds red potatoes
- 1 -tsp thyme
- Kosher salt
- 2 -tbsps olive oil
- 2 -tbsps butter
- 1/3 -mug Parmesan cheese

GUIDELINES

1. Clean and also reduced the potatoes right into quarters.

2. In a substantial dish or an extensive ziplock pack, placed the potatoes and also the rest of the repairings as well as blend/shake well.

3. Find a little bit of home heating paper in your Air Fryer.

4. Establish it to 400 ° F (200 ° C) as well as chef for 18 to 20 mins or up until the potatoes are fresh and also great.

Nourishment Info: Calories 540g, Fat 12g, Carbs 6g, Sugars 4.5 g, Healthy protein 108g

Bacon-Cheddar Stuffed Potato Skins

Servings: 4
Time: Preparation Time: 30mins, Prepare Time: 45mins

INGREDIENTS
- 2 - medium-sized russet potatoes
- olive or grease
- salt and also fresh ground black pepper
- 2 - mugs grated Cheddar cheese
- bacon
- scallions
- sour cream

DIRECTIONS
1. Pre-heat the air fryer to 400°F.
2. Cut the potatoes right into equivalent components the lengthy method, clean both sides with oil as well as period with salt and also dark pepper.
3. Exchange the potatoes, piece side as much as the air fryer container as well as air-broil at 400°F for 20 mins.
4. Turn the potatoes over as well as air-broil at 400°F for an additional 10 mins.
5. Scoop the cells out of the potato, leaving concerning 1/2- inch of the potato in the skin.
6. Brush within the potato skins with oil and also period once more with salt and also pepper. Air-broil at 400°F, skin side up, for 10 mins.
7. Load the potato skin with the ground cheddar and also bacon.

8. Return the skins to the air fryer and also air-broil at 360 ° F for 1 to 2 mins, or simply till the cheddar are liquified.
9. Leading with the hacked scallions as well as existing with severe lotion.

Nourishment Details: Calories 371.9 g, Fat 15.9 g, Carbs 43.3 g, Sugars 1.5 g, Healthy protein 17.6 g.

Steak with Baked Potatoes Ninja Style

Servings: 1.
Time: Preparation Time: 15mins, Prepare Time: 30mins.

ACTIVE INGREDIENTS
- 3 - potatoes.
- 1 - tbsp Olive Oil.
- 1 - tsp Chili pepper.
- 1 - tsp Italian Natural herbs.
- 1 - tsp Salt.
- 200g - Striploin Steak.
- 1/2 - tbsp Olive Oil.
- Salt as well as Pepper to taste.

DIRECTIONS.
1. In a tool dish, consisting of potatoes, olive oil, chili pepper, Italian natural herbs, and also salt.
2. Preheat air fryer to 180C for 5 mins.
3. Place potatoes right into air fryer container.
4. Prepare for 16 mins. Toss the potatoes midway.
5. When done, deposited.
6. Massage oil, salt, and also pepper on both sides of the steak.
7. Detect the steak right into air-fryer. Prepare at 200C for 7 to 13 mins, section upon disposition of steak doneness.
8. Existing with the simmered potatoes.

9. Value.

Nourishment Details: Calories 100.1 g, Fat 2.5 g, Carbs 18g, Sugars 1.1 g, Healthy protein 2.1 g.

Vegan / Vegetarian

Cauliflower Rice

Servings: 3
Time: Preparation Time: 10mins, Prepare Time: 20mins

INGREDIENTS
- 1/2 - block tofu
- 2 - tbsps lowered salt soy sauce
- 1/2 - mug diced onion
- 1 - mug diced carrot
- 1 - tsp turmeric extract
- 2 - tbsps lowered salt soy sauce
- 1 1/2 - tsps toasted sesame oil
- 1 - tbsp rice vinegar
- 1 - tbsp diced ginger
- 1/2 - mug carefully sliced broccoli
- 2 - cloves garlic
- 1/2 - mug icy peas

GUIDELINES
1. In a substantial dish, break down the tofu, then toss with the rest of the Round 1 correctings.
2. Air sear at 370F for 10 mins, drinking when.
3. During, toss with each other most of the Round 2 repairings in a substantial dish.
4. At the factor when that preliminary 10 mins of food preparation is done, consisting of most of the Round 2 correctings to your air fryer, tremble tenderly, as well as sear at 370 for 10 extra mins, trembling complying with 5 mins.

5. Rice cauliflower can change a whole lot in dimension, so in case you sense that your own does not look done what's required currently, you can prepare for an additional 2-5 mins at 370F. Just drink and also sign in each number of mins till it's done to your delighting in.

Nourishment Details: Calories 130g, Fat 6g, Carbs 3g, Sugars 1g, Healthy Protein 17g

Vegan Roasted Corn

Servings: 4
Time: Preparation Time: 15mins, Prepare Time: 10mins

ACTIVE INGREDIENTS
- 4 - fresh ears of corn
- 2 t o 3 - tsps grease
- salt as well as pepper to preference

GUIDELINES
1. Eliminate husks from corn, laundry as well as rub completely dry. You might require to cut the corn to suit your container.
2. In case you need to do thus, reduced the corn. Shower grease over the corn. Try to cover the corn well with the grease.
3. Period with salt as well as pepper. Prepare at 400 levels for around 10 mins.

Nourishment Details: Calories 539g, Fat 40g, Carbs 16g, Sugars 4.2 g, Healthy protein 24g

Baked Zucchini French Fries Dish

Servings: 4
Time: Preparation Time: 10mins, Prepare Time: 20mins

INGREDIENTS

- 3 - tool zucchini
- 2 - huge egg white
- 1/2 - mug skilled bread crumbs
- 2 - tablespoon grated Parmesan cheese
- cooking spray
- 1/4 - tsp garlic powder
- salt & pepper to preference

GUIDELINES

1. Identify an air conditioning shelf inside a home heating sheet as well as layer shelf with food preparation shower; deposited.
2. In a little dish, defeat egg whites as well as period with salt as well as pepper.
3. In one more dish, area breadcrumbs, garlic powder, and also cheddar as well as mix well.
4. Dive zucchini penetrates eggs after that right into bread scrap as well as cheddar mix, a pair at any type of provided minute.
5. Find the breaded zucchini in a singular layer onto the air conditioning shelf and also dash even more cooking shower on the top.
6. Prepare at 425â ° for around 15-20 mins, or up until great dark tinted.
7. Existing with Cattle ranch or Marinara sauce for diving.

Nourishment Info: Calories 83.7 g, Fat 3g, Carbs 9.4 g, Sugars 1.5 g, Healthy protein 5.1 g.

Mediterranean Veggies

Servings: 4.
Time: Preparation Time: 5mins, Prepare Time: 20mins.

INGREDIENTS

- 50g - Cherry Tomatoes.
- 1 - Huge Courgette.
- 1 - Environment-friendly Pepper.
- 1 - Huge Parsnip.
- 1 - Tool Carrot.

- 1 - Tsp Mixed Herbs.
- 2 - Tablespoon Honey.
- 1 - Tsp Mustard.
- 2 - Tsp Garlic Puree.
- 6 - Tablespoon Olive Oil.
- Salt & Pepper.
- Metric - Imperial.

DIRECTIONS.

1. In the base of your Air-fryer reduced up the courgette as well as environment-friendly pepper. Strip as well as bones the parsnip as well as carrot as well as consist of the cherry tomatoes whole while still on the creeping plant for extra taste.
2. Shower with 3 tbsps of olive oil as well as chef for 15 mins at 180c,.
3. At the same time, stimulate the rest of your correctings right into an Air-fryer secure home heating recipe.
4. At the factor when the veggies are done exchange them from the base of the Air-fryer right into the preparing meal as well as tremble well with the objective that each of the veggies is shrouded in the marinate.
5. Sprinkle with rather even more salt as well as pepper and also chef for 5 mins on 200c.

Nourishment Info: Calories 280g, Fat 21g, Carbs 21g, Sugars 13g, Healthy Protein 2g.

Breaded Mushrooms

Servings: 4.
Time: Preparation Time: 10mins, Prepare Time: 10mins.

ACTIVE INGREDIENTS.

- 250grams - Switch mushrooms.
- flour.
- 1 - egg.
- Breadcrumbs.
- 80grams - Carefully grated Parmigiano Reggiano cheese.

- salt and also pepper.

GUIDELINES.

1. In a dish, mix the breadcrumbs with the Parmigiano cheddar as well as area to the opposite side.
2. In a various dish, defeated an egg and also area to the opposite.
3. Rub dries out the mushrooms with kitchen area paper.
4. Roll the mushrooms in the flour.
5. Dunk the mushrooms in the egg.
6. Dunk the mushrooms in the breadcrumbs/cheddar mix assuring a regardless of covering.
7. Prepare in the Air-fryer on 180 levels for 7 mins. Shake when while food preparation.
8. Offer cozy with your most enjoyed diving sauce.

Nourishment Details: Calories 140g, Fat 4g, Carbs 36g, Sugars 32g, Healthy Protein 15g.

Burger District Zucchini Zircles

Servings: 3.
Time: Preparation Time: 15mins, Prepare Time: 10mins.

INGREDIENTS
- 3 - big Zucchini.
- 3/4 - mug Milk.
- 1/2 - mug All Objective Flour.
- 1 - mug Experienced Dry Italian Breadcrumbs.
- 1/2 - mug Powdered Sugar.
- Devices.
- Oil Mister.
- 1 - Fifty Percent Cookie Sheet.
- 1 - Cable Cooking Shelf.

GUIDELINES.

1. Line a Cookie Sheet with Paper Towels. Laundry as well as completely dry Zucchini. Cut Zucchini around 1/4 inch thick, comparable to Texas hold'em Chips as well as area on lined Cookie Sheet.
2. Align 3 superficial recipes, placing flour in one, milk in the adhering to as well as Seasoned Bread Crumbs in the 3rd. With one completely dry hand, layer Zucchini in flour, get rid of oversupply as well as go down right into milk. Sink/flip with a fork and also later location Zucchini in a dish with Breadcrumbs. With an additional completely dry hand, entirely layer Zucchini and also area onto Cable Cooking Shelf.
3. In a singular layer, tenderly area Zucchini Zircles in arranged/lubed Air Fryer Basket as well as use an Oil Mister to sprinkle well with Oil.
4. Prepare at 390 levels for 8 mins, carefully turning one-part of the method via.
5. Eliminate from Air Fryer as well as spray with Powdered Sugar. Existing with Burger

Nourishment Details: Calories 80g, Fat 2g, Carbs 16g, Sugars 12g, Healthy protein 23.5 g.

Air-Fried Asparagus

Serving: 4

Time: Prep Time: 5mins, Cook Time: 10mins

Fixings
- ½ - pack of asparagus
- Avocado or Olive Oil
- Himalayan salt
- Dark pepper

Directions

1. Spot cut asparagus sticks perceptible all around fryer bushel. Spritz sticks delicately with oil, by then sprinkle with salt and a little bit of dull pepper.
2. Spot container inside air-fryer and warmth at 400° for 10 minutes.
3. Serve immediately.

Nourishment Information: Calories 229.6g, Fat 8.1g, Carbs 11g, Sugars 1g, Protein 26.2g

Roasted Broccoli

Serving: 2
Time: Prep Time: 45mins, Cook Time: 10mins

INGREDIENTS
500grams broccoli

For marinade
- 2 - tbsp yogurt
- 1 - tbsp chickpea flour
- ¼ - tsp turmeric powder
- ½ - tsp salt
- ½ - tsp red stew powder
- ¼ - tsp masala talk

DIRECTIONS

1. To arrangement firm stewed broccoli, we should decrease the broccoli into little florets.
2. Absorb a bowl of water with 2 tsp salt for half-hour to remove any dirtying effects or worms.
3. Expel the broccoli florets from the water. Channel pleasantly and wipe through and through utilizing a kitchen towel to absorb all the soddenness.
4. In a bowl, incorporate all of the components for the marinade.

5. Hurl the broccoli florets on this marinade. Spread and hold aside inside the refrigerator for 15 minutes.
6. At the factor while the broccoli is marinated, preheat the air-fryer at 2 100°C.
7. Open the bushel of the air-fryer and see the marinated florets inside. Drive the canister back in, and flip the time dial to 10mins.
8. Give the bushel a shake once halfway and later on investigate following 10mins if mind blowing and new. In the event that never again, safeguard for some other 2-3mins. Eat them warm!
9. On the off risk which you don't have an air-fryer, use a preheated grill and spread the florets on a lined getting ready plate and warmth for round 15mins in a preheated stove at one hundred 90°C or till radiant and new.

Nutrition Information: Calories 120g, Fat 7.4g, Carbs 28g, Sugars 24g, Protein 21g

Sweet Cooked Carrots

Serving: 4
Time: Prep Time: 15mins, Cook Time: 10mins

INGREDIENTS
- 3 - measures of infant carrots
- 1 - tbsp Olive oil
- 1 - tbsp Honey
- Salt and pepper to taste

GUIDELINES

1. In a bowl, mix the carrots with the nectar and the olive oil.
2. Guarantee carrots are all around verified.
3. Season with salt and pepper.
4. Cook in the Air-fryer on 200 degrees for 12 minutes.

5. Serve hot.

Nutrition Information: Calories 200g, Fat 8.3g, Carbs 44g, Sugars 40g, Protein 14.2g

Mac and Cheese

Serving: 4
Time: Prep Time: 15mins, Cook Time: 20mins

INGREDIENTS
- 1 - glass Elbow Macaroni
- ½ - glass Broccoli
- ½ - glass Milk
- 1 ½ - glass Cheddar Cheese
- Salt
- Pepper
- 1 - tbsp Parmesan Cheese

DIRECTIONS

1. Preheat the Air-fryer at 200°C. Pass on a pot of water to rise over high hears, decrease the glow to medium and incorporate macaroni and vegetables. Stew until macaroni is still to some degree firm and vegetables are sensitive anyway not delicate. Channel pasta and vegetables and return them to pot.

2. Add milk and cheddar to the macaroni and vegetables, and throw to join. Season with pepper and salt.

3. Empty pasta mix into an ovenproof dish. Sprinkle the Parmesan cheddar over top. Detect the dish detailing progressively fryer receptacle and change the temperature to 180°C and heat for 15 minutes. Grant to sit for 5-10 minutes in the Air-fryer before serving.

Nutrition Information: Calories 65g, Fat 22g, Carbs 10g, Sugars 10g, Protein 11.2g

Veggie lover Cheesy Potato Wedges

Serving: 4
Time: Prep Time: 15mins, Cook Time: 20mins

INGREDIENTS

For the Potatoes
- 1 - lb fingerling potatoes
- 1 - tsp additional virgin olive oil
- 1 - tsp legitimate salt
- 1 - tsp ground dark pepper
- ½ - tsp garlic powder

For the Cheese Sauce
- ½ - container crude cashews
- ½ - tstp ground turmeric
- ½ - tsp paprika
- 2 - TB dietary yeast
- 1 - tsp new lemon juice
- 2 - tablespoons to 1/4 container water

DIRECTIONS
1. Preheat the air fryer to four hundred°F for three minutes. Wash the potatoes.
2. Cut the potatoes down the middle longwise and interchange them to a bowl.
3. Include the oil, salt, pepper, and garlic powder to the potatoes.
4. Exchange the potatoes to the air fryer. Cook for 16mins, shaking some portion of the way by means of the cooking time.
5. Consolidate the cashews, turmeric, paprika, solid yeast, and lemon crush in a fast blender.
6. Mix on low, bit by bit expanding the speed and which incorporate water.

7. Be careful so as to keep away from utilizing a lot of water, as you need a thick, smooth consistency.

8. Exchange the cooked potatoes to an air fryer–safe field or a piece of fabric paper.

9. Shower the cheddar sauce over the potato wedges. Recognize the dish incredible all around fryer and cook supper for 2mins at 400°F.

Nutrition Information: Calories 220g, Fat 8g, Carbs 30g, Sugar 12g, Protein 7.5g

Avocado Egg Rolls with Chili Sauce

Servings: 5
Time: Preparation Time: 20mins, Prepare Time: 25mins

ACTIVE INGREDIENTS

- 10 - egg roll wrappers
- 3 - avocados peeled off and also matched
- 1 - Roma tomato diced
- 1/2 - tsp salt
- 1/4 - tsp pepper
- canola oil for frying
- For the wonderful chili sauce:
- 4 - tbsps sriracha
- 2 - tbsps white sugar
- 1 - tbsp rice vinegar
- 1 - tbsp sesame oil

GUIDELINES

1. Consist of avocados, tomato, salt, as well as pepper to a blending dish. Squash the avocados to a thick uniformity and also mix to sign up with the dealings with.

2. This will certainly become being the egg pass dental filling.

3. Expand the egg circulation wrappers and also a touch dish of water.

4. Communicate the egg distribute filling up the numerous wrappers, scooping them onto the lower 3rd of every wrapper.

5. Taking one wrapper right away, take advantage of a finger to move water along with its 4 sides. Wrinkle up a space over the dental filling, at that aspect the sides, and also afterwards flow it up. Touch the last overlay with added water to seal. Rehash for each single various wrapper.

6. Include canola oil to a large pot till the oil is around 2 inches down.

7. Transform the heater to tool heat. At the factor while the oil temperature level accomplishes 350 F, consist of the egg is offered in numbers.

8. Prepare up until fantastic darkish tinted, rounded 3 mins. Exchange to a paper towel to consume. Cut every egg roll space to space.

9. Combine sauce correctings in a little bit dish. Mix perfectly. Existing with lower avocado egg rolls.

Nourishment Info: Calories 293g, Fat 16g, Carbs 25.3 g, Sugars 4g, Healthy protein 13.3 g.

Garlic Baked Mushrooms

Servings: 4.
Time: Preparation Time: 10mins, Prepare Time: 30mins.

ACTIVE INGREDIENTS
- 1kg - mushrooms.
- 1 - tablespoon duck fat.
- 1/2 - tsp garlic powder.
- 2 - tsps herbes de provence.
- 2 - tbsps white vermouth.

DIRECTIONS

1. Clean the mushrooms; transform completely dry in an offering of blended environment-friendlies rewriter, quarter them and also deposit.

2. Place the duck fat, the garlic powder, and also the herbes de provence in the container of your oar. Heat for 2 mins. Combine with a wood spoon on the occasion that it gathered.

3. Consist of the mushrooms, chef for 25 mins. Consist of the white vermouth, chef for an added 5 mins.

Nourishment Details: Calories 210g, Fat 11g, Carbs 63g, Sugars 60g, Healthy protein 14.3 g.

Air Fryer Buffalo Cauliflower

Servings: 4.
Time: Preparation Time: 20mins, Prepare Time: 30mins.

ACTIVE INGREDIENTS
- 1 - average head cauliflower.
- 1 1/2 - florets.
- 2-3 - tbsps Frank's Red Hot Sauce.
- 1 1/2 - tsps maple syrup.
- 2 - tsps avocado oil.
- 2-3 - tbsps dietary yeast.
- 1/4 - tsp sea salt1 tbsp corn starch.

INSTRUCTIONS
1. Establish air fryer to 360 degrees F. Include all mendings other than cauliflower to a large mixing dish. Race to combine definitely.
2. Include cauliflower as well as toss to layer consistently.
3. Include 1/2 of your cauliflower to air fryer. Prepare for 12-14 mins, trembling midway, or till you get desired uniformity.
4. Rehash with recurring cauliflower, in addition to reduction chef supper time to 9-10mins.

5. Cauliflower will certainly preserve securely dealt with within the refrigerator as long as 4 days. To warm, include once more to air fryer for 1-2 mins, till heated using as well as actually business.

Nourishment Info: Calories 345g, Fat 17g, Carbs 41g, Sugars 21g, Healthy Protein 12g.

Thai Coconut Veggie Bites

Serving: 16
Time: Prep Time: 5mins, Cook Time: 20mins

INGREDIENTS
- 1 - Large Broccoli
- 1 - Large Cauliflower
- 6 - Large Carrots
- Bunch Garden Peas
- ½ - Cauliflower made into cauliflower rice
- 1 - Large Onion stripped and diced
- 1 - Small Courgette
- 2 - Leeks cleaned and meagerly cut
- 1 - Can Coconut Milk
- 50g - Plain Flour
- 1 - cm Cube Ginger stripped and ground
- 1 - Tbsp Garlic Puree
- 1 - Tbsp Olive Oil
- 1 - Tbsp Thai Green Curry Paste
- 1 - Tbsp Coriander
- 1 - Tbsp Mixed Spice
- 1 - Tsp Cumin
- Salt and Pepper

DIRECTIONS
1. In a wok cook your onion with the garlic, ginger and olive oil until the onion has an OK bit of shading on it.
2. While you are cooking your onion in a steamer cook your vegetables for 20 minutes or until they are nearly cooked.

3. Include the courgette, the leek and the curry paste to your work and cook on a medium warmth for a further 5 minutes.

4. Include the coconut milk and the rest of the seasoning mix well and after that incorporate the cauliflower rice.

5. Blend again and license stewing for 10 minutes.

6. When it has stewed for 10 minutes and the sauce has lessened significantly, incorporate the steamed vegetables.

7. Blend well and you will by and by have a shocking base for your veggie snack.

8. A spot in the refrigerator for an hour to allow to cool.

9. Following an hour make into snack sizes and spot in the Air Fryer. Cook for 10 minutes at 180c and a short time later present with a cooling dive.

Nutrition Information: Calories 117g, Fat 7g, Carbs 12g, Sugar 3g, Protein 2g

Garlic and Herb Roasted Chickpeas

Serving: 4
Time: Prep Time: 5mins, Cook Time: 20mins

INGREDIENTS
2 - jars of chickpeas
1 - tbsp olive oil
1 - tbsp nourishing yeast
2 - tsp garlic powder
1 - tbsp blended herbs
Ocean salt and dark pepper to taste

DIRECTIONS

1. Channel and wash the chickpeas, by then add to a medium-sized mixing bowl and incorporate the olive oil and seasonings.

2. Blend well to join using a spatula, ensuring all chickpeas are all around secured.

3. Gap and cook in two bunches recognizable all around fryer at 200°C for 15-20 minutes, mixing once at the 10-minute engraving.

4. You may hear some popping while they're cooking which is completely common. They're done once they're splendid darker and firm al the way through.

5. Serve while warm and store in a water/air evidence compartment once cooled to ensure freshness.

Nutrition Information: Calories 387g, Fat 21g, Carbs 48g, Sugars 8g, Protein 9g

Spicy Cauliflower Stir-Fry

Serving: 4
Time: Prep Time: 10mins, Cook Time: 25mins

INGREDIENTS
- 1 - head cauliflower
- ¾ - glass onion white
- 5 - cloves garlic
- 1 ½ - tablespoons tamari
- 1 - tablespoon rice vinegar
- ½ - teaspoon coconut sugar
- 1 - tablespoon Sriracha
- 2 - scallions for enhancement

DIRECTIONS

1. Spot cauliflower recognizable all around fryer. In case your air fryer is one that has openings in the base, you'll need to use an air fryer install.

2. Set the temp to 350 degrees. Cook 10 minutes.

Conclusion

I want to thank you for downloading my book *Ninja Foodi: The Complete Recipes Cookbook*. I take great pleasure in cooking and bringing you the best of my home cooking there is.

Remember to have fun and enjoy your cooking and live life to the fullest. Have a fantastic day! Bye

Daniel Rowley

Lightning Source UK Ltd.
Milton Keynes UK
UKHW050946300421
382900UK00009B/277